IN HEROES' FOOTSTEPS

IN HEROES' FOOTSTEPS

A WALKER'S GUIDE TO THE BATTLEFIELDS OF THE WORLD

TIM NEWARK

NEW BURLINGTON BOOKS

A QUARTO BOOK

First published in 2001 by New Burlington Books
6 Blundell Street
London N7 9BH

ISBN 1-86155-590-3

QUAR.HFO

Conceived, designed, and produced by
Quarto Publishing plc
The Old Brewery
6 Blundell Street
London
N7 9BH

Editors Kate Michell
Paula Regan
Text editor Peter Kirkham
Indexer Dorothy Frame

Art Director Moira Clinch

Art Editor Elizabeth Healey
Designer Malcolm Smyth
Photographer Ian Howes
Cartographer Malcolm Swanston

Publisher Piers Spence

Manufactured in China by Regent Publishing Services, Limited
Printed in China by Midas Printing Limited

CONTENTS

IMPERIAL
WAR MUSEUM
HEN·VIII·REGE·FVNDATVM·CIVIVM·LARGITAS·PERFECIT·

LANDSCAPE OF WAR

Above *Re-enactors can never recreate the experience of battle,* *but they can tell you something about the material sensation of being a soldier, such as how heavy armor is or what it is like to fire a musket.*

Left *The Imperial War Museum* *in London. One of the great military museums of the world, it combines remarkable objects of war with the personal reminiscences of soldiers and civilians.*

Battlefields are extraordinary places. For a few hours, perhaps a few days, they are the location of trauma on a massive scale. Thousands of soldiers, and frequently civilians, face and endure savage injury and death. A myriad of lives are disrupted, minds are in turmoil, bodies vulnerable and fragmented. It is a horrible, frightening place to be, the worst we can imagine—and then, all is quiet. The battle ceases and nature returns, covering the churned earth with grass and weeds, covering the bones of the dead with flowers and trees.

IMAGINATION

Trying to conceive what it was like at the time of battle is the supreme act of imagination. It requires research and empathy, and hopefully this book will provide a beginning in that process. In addition to reading books and visiting museums, it is also worthwhile to talk to re-enactors who sometimes perform on or near these battlefields. Not because they can convey the experience of being in a battle—they cannot—but they can give clues to what the material sensation was like: what a uniform feels like, how heavy a sword is, the process of loading and firing a musket.

"To wear a cloak and sword makes you feel different," concludes Dr. Simon James of Leeds School of Archaeology. "You have a different sense of yourself—you even walk differently. That helps you get a little more into the mind of early medieval warriors." The same is true of uniforms that were designed to shape the body and make the wearer feel more like a member of a martial community. They helped to ready raw recruits for the process of battle.

"We have certainly discovered how little we know," says Graham Sumner, a member of the Ermine Street Guard. "Roman soldiers appear to have been trained in gladiatorial forms of combat, but these seem inappropriate to the battlefield. On the other hand, what we have recreated is the noise of a legion on the move. Groups of legionnaires marching in full armor make such a noise that we have concluded that visual and not verbal commands would have been used—musicians and standard-bearers being used to convey these to ranks of soldiers deafened by the sound of their own clanging arms and armor."

TALKING TO VETERANS

Most useful of all is to talk to veterans, listening to the incidental details of recruitment and training, as well as the front-line anecdotes. How they cope with the fear that grips anyone in these situations reveals the humanity of the moment. John Wright was a sapper (a specialist in field fortifications or demolition) and officer who fought in ten battles throughout World War II, in Egypt, India, and Burma, including the savage siege of Kohima. He disagrees with the theory that courage is worn down over time. "Experience and battle sense, reading the battle," he says, "sharpens one's grasp of an otherwise confusing situation, to the extent that one no longer worries needlessly over apparent threats that are in fact relatively innocuous." This included airstrikes, which he says sounded far worse than they were on the ground.

Good leadership is crucial. "It bolsters the morale and shows what can be achieved through mutual trust," remembers Wright. "The Sher Regiment had Gurkha troops but poor officers. All 730 of them ran through us when mortared and probably incurred more casualties then than we did over the eighteen or so days of being under continuous attack." Fear of letting your comrades down is important too, especially if you are an officer. "Interdependence with companions boosts one's confidence as well as one's concern to be dependable on their behalf. All of which tends to grow with time."

Not all veterans of conflict are front-line soldiers. In the twentieth century, through the aerial bombing of cities, civilians have found themselves in the middle of battles. Talking to parents and grandparents sometimes reveals how ordinary life can clash with sudden danger. While bombs rained down on London during the Blitz, my mother recalls as a teenage girl refusing to go into the air-raid shelter built in her back garden. "I couldn't stand this. It smelled terrible and my mother and father would always be arguing. I preferred to stay in the house and face the Luftwaffe, than go in that tiny hole with my family."

Civilians became primary targets in war *in the twentieth century. Rescue workers search for survivors in a house wrecked by the German bombing of Dover of 1943.*

INVISIBLE BATTLEFIELDS

Muddy fields and empty trenches are easier to transform in our minds into the scenes of battles, but nine out of the seventeen battles featured in this book were fought in or around settlements. Some of these battles even resulted in the devastation of major cities. Sieges were a familiar part of medieval and early modern warfare, but there were usually rough and ready rules to these engagements, in which the majority of the fighting was undertaken by soldiers manning the walls of towns, and if the town surrendered, the civilian population would be spared.

In the twentieth century, a new kind of warfare took hold in which civilians became the primary target of attack in an effort to reduce the morale of the nation as a whole. Germany took the lead in this form of total warfare with the aerial bombing of major cities throughout Western and Eastern Europe. Warsaw was very nearly annihilated and London suffered badly. In retaliation, Berlin became the victim of both Allied and Soviet bombing. Today, these battlefields are almost invisible.

In defiance of the German brutality visited on their people and city, the citizens of Warsaw have rebuilt their Old Town so that walking around it now, it is hard to believe that the baroque merchants' houses and glorious town squares are not at least 300 years old, rather than fifty. In London, there was less reconstruction, more a wish to look to the future and create a new city of modern buildings. In Berlin, the core of the city that had housed Hitler and his Nazi supporters was for a long time a wasteland with the Berlin Wall running through the middle of it. Only recently, with German reunification and the end of the Cold War, has a new city been allowed to rise on the ground of the final battle.

Statue of Bismarck, chancellor of Prussia *during its unification of Germany in the late nineteenth century, now standing in the Tiergarten in Berlin. Statues of kings and commanders were the first forms of war monuments, but the terrible casualties of World War I saw a demand in statues remembering the ordinary soldier.*

MONUMENTS TO WAR

As the urban scars of battle disappear, other elements are needed to remind citizens and tourists of the violent events that happened on the streets around them. Monuments are an important aspect of this collective memory. In Warsaw, the Old Town was very quickly rebuilt after World War II, but monuments did not feature highly in this process, possibly because the new Soviet-backed Communist masters of the city wished to begin their regime without any reference to the past. Monuments to the Warsaw Uprising would only stimulate feelings of national resistance which might be directed at the Communists. So, eerily, the dreadful events of the German occupation survived largely in the minds of those who suffered it, while around them a new city arose, blotting out the past. With the collapse of the Soviet Union and communism in Poland, dramatic new monuments to the Warsaw Uprising were erected, and these form important focal points for acts of remembrance, even contrition by German politicians.

In Western Europe, war monuments have a long tradition, being first raised during the Renaissance, when the Classical fashion for erecting public statues was revived. At first, these monuments recalled

Canadian Monument at Vimy Ridge, *a thoughtful memorial in contrast to the triumphant statues of an earlier age.*

great men, such as kings and generals. Then there were emblematic monuments that chose symbols of victory or resistance, Michelangelo's *David* being an early example of a figure chosen to represent Florence's defiance of its larger neighbors.

In Berlin, in the late nineteenth century, both kinds of monuments were featured with statues to the leading generals of Prussia's victories being raised in the *Tiergarten* (zoological garden), while the main object of veneration was the *Siegessaule* or Victory Column. At its summit was the winged personification of victory, while on its column were the gilded barrels of cannons captured from the French. Metal friezes at its base show scenes of Prussian battle success. It is a striking monument to German arrogance at the time, that surprisingly was not destroyed when the Soviets captured Berlin. The scars of battle clearly visible on its marble base make the *Siegessaule* perhaps the first ironic monument to battle.

ORDINARY SOLDIERS

World War I changed the public attitude to war monuments. So many ordinary soldiers had died in the trauma of the Western Front, that people wanted to remember them, rather than the generals and politicians who had directed them. Throughout Britain, monuments listing the names of all those who had sacrificed their lives in the war, were raised in almost every town. No longer would ordinary soldiers be anonymous, their identities lost on a distant battlefield. They would be remembered at home forever. Even those soldiers whose bodies were eradicated by modern weapons would be commemorated by the Tomb of the Unknown Soldier, and their sacrifice would be remembered every November at the Cenotaph in Whitehall, a suitably abstract piece of architecture.

Perhaps the most moving monument erected in London to this new spirit of remembrance is the Royal Artillery monument at Hyde Park Corner. Designed by Charles Sargeant Jagger in 1925, it features a massive stone howitzer, surrounded by four larger-than-life sculptures of Royal Artillery soldiers. Rather than being shown as classical heroes, these are portraits of real men weighed down with uniforms and pieces of equipment. They are heroic, but in a quiet, enduring, realistic way, as soldiers really are.

When World War II ended, many of the monuments from World War I were used again, with new panels adding news lists of names to be remembered.

Royal Artillery monument in London, *designed by Charles Sargeant Jagger in 1925. One of the best memorials to soldiers ever built, it portrays their quiet heroism by showing them loaded with the equipment of war.*

Some minor new monuments were raised, but on the whole, it seems that government and local authorities have hoped that the memories of all those involved, civilians included, will serve as a more potent memorial. As the years go by and veterans pass away, this hope is not good enough. Cities are tough and quickly shrug off assaults by war, but their citizens should not do likewise and many war-savaged cities should think about following the example of Warsaw and build major new memorials. Who will soon remember the Blitz and the deaths of 43,000 men, women, and children—most of them killed in or near their homes? Time should not heal these particular wounds.

MOVIE LEGENDS

Battlefields and monuments are not the only ways of contacting the past. At least three of the battles featured in this book have been the subject of popular celebration. The battles of Little Bighorn, Rorke's Drift, and the Charge of the Light Brigade, all caught the imagination of people at the time, and the tales of courage that have arisen out of them have endured for over a hundred years, being portrayed in epic paintings and dramatic films. Curiously, only one of these battles was a victory for the audience celebrating them. Little Bighorn was a defeat for white Americans, while the Charge of the Light Brigade was a failure for Victorian Britain, but this seems less important than the fact that soldiers were shown to have bravely performed their duty in desperate situations.

Movies that celebrate military virtues are frequently condemned as unrealistic or somehow promoting war. However, there are some that recognize the very highest of human qualities and this should put them in the first rank of artistic achievement. But such are intellectual prejudices since World War I that any portrayal of battle is perceived as bad. This attitude reached its climax in the 1970s when the Vietnam War became the setting for tales of disillusion and cynicism.

A decade earlier, the motion picture *Zulu* had portrayed a small group of soldiers showing remarkable bravery in the face of overwhelming odds. Similar events occurred in the Vietnam War, particularly during the battle of Hue featured in this book, but to have portrayed them in a movie in the 1970s would have been to invite derision. The American media and intelligentsia were so anti-war that they grossly misrepresented what actually happened. This did a great disservice to the soldiers who fought there and only recently has this condemnation been slowly overcome by books and films portraying a truer picture. And yet, war movies are still made under a cloud of disapproval. This is a great shame for they serve a cultural purpose as important as the ancient sculptures on the Parthenon in Athens, showing that even in war human beings can act with nobility and bravery and that their sacrifices should never be forgotten.

Recreated 17th Lancer in action *from the 1968 film* Charge of the Light Brigade. *Already a Victorian icon of duty in the face of death, it later became a symbol of courage despite calamity.*

NORTH AMERICA

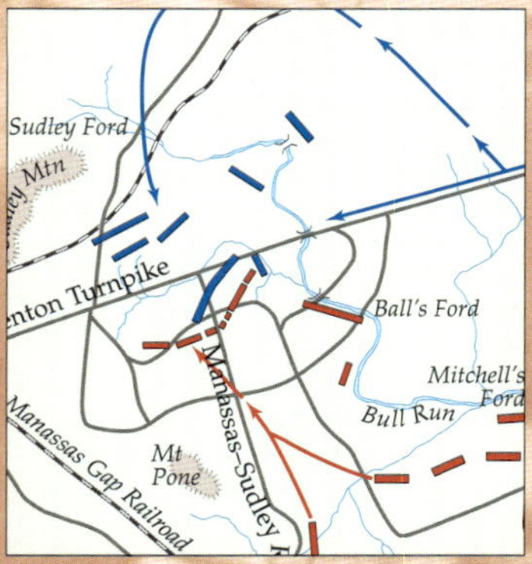

The story of the fight for independence is never far from the landscape of North America, whether it be the clash of two great powers in the war of 1812 at Fort George, or the last battle for survival of the Native American tribes at Little Bighorn.

Dominating them all is the great Civil War fought between two cultures, each with a different vision of its own liberty. When the fighting was over, the battlefields became sacred land to remind their people that such sacrifices should never be entered into lightly.

CONQUER CANADA!

Above ***Contemporary cartoon*** *showing the English King George III embroiled in the War of 1812 "in mud up to his ears," caught between a Kentucky rifleman and a Louisiana Creole.*

Left ***American troops advance*** *at the battle of Chippewa in July 1814, which saw a resurgent U.S. army beat the British and force them back along the Niagara River toward Fort George.*

The New Republic of the United States of America was in an aggressive mood in the summer of 1812. Americans were fed up with British arrogance at sea and believed the British were inciting Indian raids on white settlers. With the majority of British forces committed to a war against Napoleon in Europe, it seemed the right time to declare war on their former colonial master and claim the land of Canada for their own—fewer than 6,000 British soldiers defended it. This was also an election year and President James Madison won another term with his aggressive stance. However, the U.S. army was not prepared for an invasion of Canada and the first year's campaigning ended in humiliating failure.

GUARDIAN FORTS

The key to Canada was mastery of the rivers and lakes that led to it from the United States. The Niagara River ran from Lake Erie to Lake Ontario, but the entrance to Lake Ontario was guarded by two forts overlooking the Niagara, both in British hands—Fort Niagara and Fort George. Built between 1796 and 1799, Fort George was the first fort to be encountered along the Niagara River and served as a dominant defensive position, protecting the nearby settlement of Newark. Its wood and earth ramparts were defended by all forms of artillery, including Congreve rockets and a well-trained, well-supplied garrison of redcoats under the

BACKGROUND TO BATTLE

The War of 1812 seems borne out of arrogance on both sides. The British believed they could do whatever they wanted on the high seas and, increasingly, their ships would stop American merchantmen to search for deserters. If they failed to find them, they would impress American seamen. Some 6,000 Americans were forced into serving in the Royal Navy during that period.

In their turn, the Americans believed it would be easy to take Canada from the British. Perhaps relying too much on memories of the War of Independence, the U.S. army was wholly unprepared for war and lost Detroit without firing a shot. President James Madison had hoped to settle the disputes by diplomacy, but hawkish politicians such as Henry Clay and John C. Calhoun forced through a declaration of war.

In the event, the two sides were too evenly balanced for one to win a great advantage over the other. With the end of the war against Napoleon in 1814, Britain could bring its full power to bear on the United States. However, by then the mood was ripe for reconciliation, although, ironically, the greatest U.S. victory of the war, at the battle of New Orleans, was won after the peace was signed.

command of Major General Isaac Brock.

By 1813 the Americans had learned from their amateurish beginning to the war, and now mounted a more aggressive assault on Canada. U.S. ships took command of Lake Erie and clashed with British ships, gaining a victory that surprised the British who were so used to naval mastery. By winning control of Lake Erie, the Americans severed the supply route to Detroit, which the British had earlier gained in the war. The British were now on the defensive and had to retreat to the west coast of Lake Ontario. It was hard for the Indian allies of the British to accept that a naval clash many miles away should effect their possession of land, and the decision to retreat lost the British some Indian support.

ABOVE *Indian warriors attack U.S. soldiers* *in support of the British army during the War of 1812.*

On Lake Ontario there was a race to outbuild each other with ships, but neither side gained dominance. Without British naval superiority in the area, the British forts along the Niagara River became vulnerable and, in May 1813, American forces decided to exploit this weakness. U.S. ships sailed along the river and bombarded Fort George. Its guns were not sufficient to counter the combination of warship broadsides and artillery batteries, and it was reduced to ruins. The outnumbered British garrison was forced to retreat, and the Americans occupied the fort throughout the

A NEAR MISS

In the summer of 1814, U.S. army Drummer Hanks recalls the firepower unleashed by the British garrison at Fort George as the U.S. army tried to provoke its defenders into attacking them. He describes an artillery shell being fired from the fort:

"In a moment we all saw it, and heard it buzzing through the air and were all upon the lookout to ascertain where it was going to fall. [Brigadier] General [Winfield] Scott threw up his sword, in such a manner as to take sight across it, at the bomb, and found that it would fall upon him and his charger, unless he made his escape instantly. He wheeled his spirited animal to the left, and buried his spurs in his sides. The whole army was gazing on the scene...when the shell actually dropped upon the very spot he had a moment before occupied."

Quoted in WHERE RIGHT AND GLORY LEAD! *by Donald E. Graves (Robin Brass, Toronto, 1997).*

Naval cannon pointing *through a section of reconstructed wall at Fort George. (Photo by Alec Hasenson.)*

Above ***Reconstructed blockhouse*** *inside Fort George used as a barracks for the British garrison. Built of heavy, white, pine logs, this building was safe against artillery shrapnel. If the palisades were overrun, it would be the last line of defense, with muskets fired through slits in the walls. (Photo by Alec Hasenson.)*

Below ***British forces set light*** *to American towns, including Washington D.C. in August 1814 , in retaliation for the American burning of Newark near Fort George and other Canadian settlements.*

summer and fall of 1813, repairing the damage that they, themselves, had inflicted on it.

BRITISH RETURN

Despite encouraging U.S. successes in the summer of 1813, the American and British forces were too evenly balanced for either side to gain any advantage in the Niagara region. American forces were too few in number to organize an effective invasion of Canada. In contrast, the British had raised a very effective local militia called the Canadian Fencibles. These troops soon proved themselves the equal of British redcoats and helped defeat U.S. soldiers in clash after clash.

With the weather deteriorating, the Americans were forced to abandon Fort George, but burned the settlement of Newark before they left. The burning of this and other Canadian settlements by the Americans became the excuse for the retaliatory British destruction of American towns, culminating in the burning

of Washington, D.C. in August 1814. The Americans retreated to Fort Niagara, but the British surged onward and took that prize also.

The war carried on into 1814. It did not look good for the Americans. The war against Napoleon had ended in Europe and this freed British soldiers to sail to Canada. The British also had more ships available and increased their blockade of American ports. But despite gaining numerical superiority, the British faced a more experienced U.S. army and, in the summer of 1814, the Americans took Fort Erie. Under the command of Major General Jacob Brown, they defeated the British at the battle of Chippewa on July 5. They surged back into the Niagara region and considered retaking Fort George.

ABOVE *Recreated private of the Eighth (King's) Regiment of Foot* *about to fire his "Brown Bess" musket inside Fort George. (Photo by Alec Hasenson.)*

Brown lingered at Fort George, and the British bravely sallied out to change his mind. They were determined not to give up Fort George and fired an impressive array of artillery. According to one eyewitness: "Our first look [at the fort] was within range of Congreve rockets, bombshells, and large shot, all seasoned with a sprinkling of grape and canister."

With no heavy artillery to break the British defenses and failing to draw them into a battle, Brown retreated to Queenston. The bloodiest battle of the war then followed at Lundy's Lane on July 25, but, though they fought well and hard, the Americans had to withdraw further, blowing up Fort Erie on the way and retreating to their own territory. With major reinforcements, the British took the war to the United States. A U.S. naval victory on Lake Champlain halted the British invasion, but the Americans were ready to enter peace negotiations and the war ended on Christmas Eve 1814. As for gallant Fort George, the British decided to build a new fort of Mississauga at the mouth of the Niagara River, and Fort George was allowed to fall into ruin, finally being abandoned in the late 1820s.

BELOW *A line of British redcoats* *advancing on the Americans is recreated inside Fort George. (Photo by Alec Hasenson.)*

BELOW *Re-enactors recreate a line of fire* *of the Sixth U.S. Infantry Regiment inside Fort George. (Photo by Alec Hasenson.)*

FORT GEORGE

***Battle of Queenston on the Niagara river** on October 13, 1812, one of the first battles along this strategically important waterway guarded by Fort George. British soldiers advance across the river in rowing boats.*

Fort George is now a Canadian national historic site. Restored to its former glory in 1950, it gives an accurate impression of an early nineteenth-century fort, typical of the forts that defended the British colony during the War of 1812. The entrance to the fort is guarded by a massive timber gate, reinforced with iron spikes. In front of the gate is a v-shaped earthwork called a ravelin, which served to break any attacking troops into two streams that would then have to face artillery mounted on the bastions on either side of the entrance. Inside the fort, visitors were required to stop at the guardhouse. The garrison guards rested here between shifts, and directly outside was the punishment area where offenders were flogged. Officers were quartered in more elegant surroundings and dined well with china and silverware imported from England. Other buildings include workshops for craftsmen such as carpenters and blacksmiths, who were essential for the maintenance of the fort.

The powder magazine is the only building to survive from the original fort and contained several hundred barrels of gunpowder during the War of 1812. Despite the thick earthen banks surrounding it, a direct shot from American gunners penetrated it in 1812 and the entire fort had to be hastily evacuated as they feared 800 barrels of gunpowder exploding. A brave group of local militiamen and royal artillerymen stayed to extinguish the fire before it ignited the gunpowder.

PLAN OF BATTLE

If the United States wished to invade British Canada during the War of 1812, then first it had to master the Great Lakes. Much fighting took place on Lake Erie and Lake Ontario and the Americans were fortunate to win more naval confrontations than the British, shaking British belief in their own naval supremacy. With the lakes mastered, American or British land forces could then advance along the Niagara river and deal with the forts that dominated the river ways.

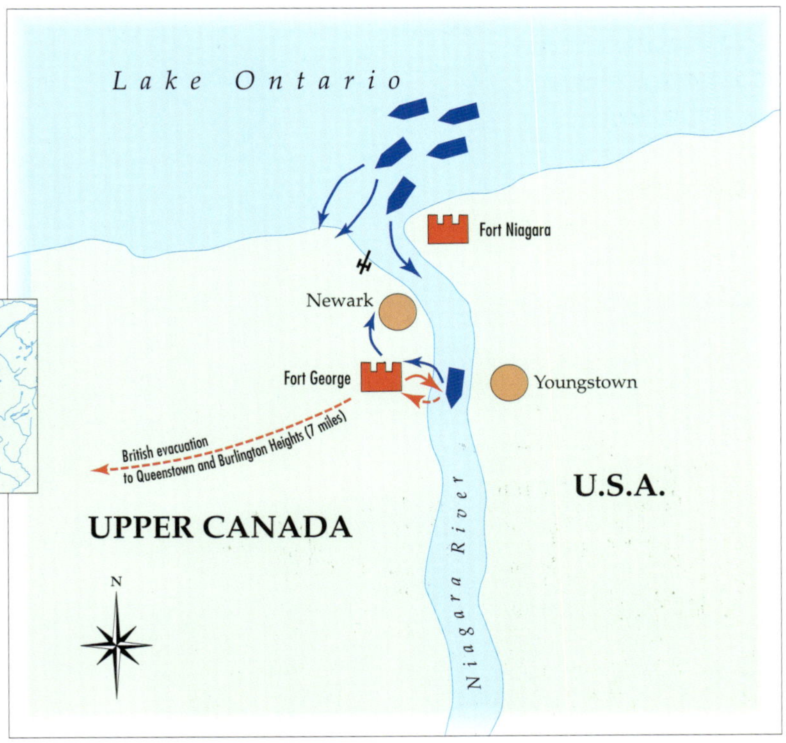

FORT GEORGE

NOT FAR FROM NIAGARA FALLS, a visit to Fort George makes an excellent day out with frequent re-enactments adding to the early nineteenth-century atmosphere of the reconstructed settlement.

BROCK'S BASTION

Another vital bastion (9), heavy artillery from here could reach the heart of Fort Niagara and controlled the entrance to Niagara river. It was named after the commander Major General Isaac Brock, who died during the battle of Queenston Heights in 1812 and was buried here.

ABOVE ***Native American*** *of the type that supported Britain in the War of 1812, recreated by an actor inside Fort George. (Photo by Alec Hasenson.)*

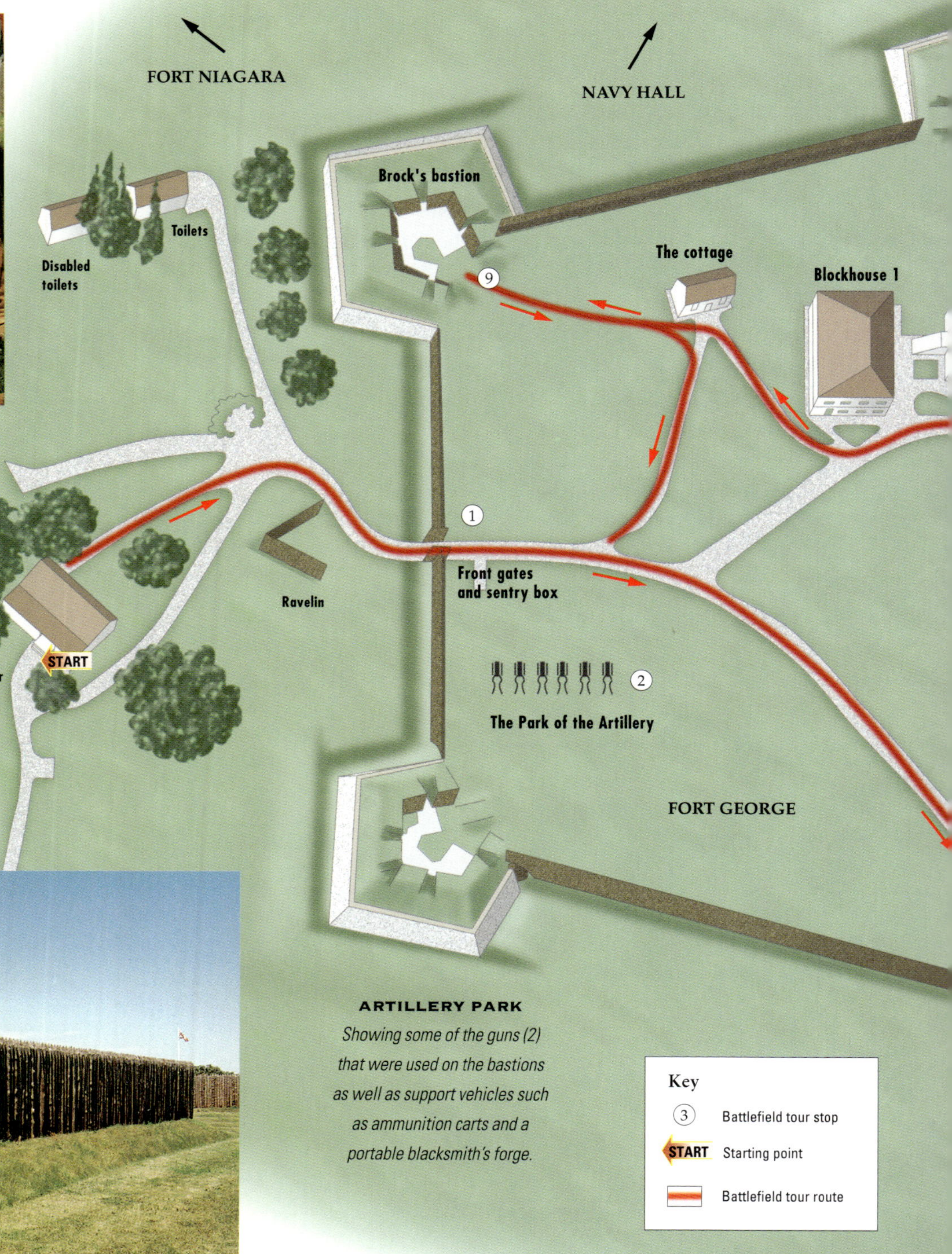

ENTRANCE TO FORT GEORGE

Massive timber gate (1) reinforced with iron spikes and ravelin earthwork in front of it.

ARTILLERY PARK

Showing some of the guns (2) that were used on the bastions as well as support vehicles such as ammunition carts and a portable blacksmith's forge.

BELOW ***Exterior view*** *of the reconstructed wooden palisades that surrounded Fort George. (Photo by Alec Hasenson.)*

FLAG BASTION

Biggest and most heavily armed of the bastions (8) overlooking the Niagara river. Below it stretched the storehouses and wharves of Navy Hall, the British naval headquarters for the Great Lakes fleet. This was destroyed by the Americans during the War of 1812.

ABOVE *Field artillery gun* *of the sort used to defend Fort George being rushed through by re-enactors. (Photo by Alec Hasenson.)*

GETTING THERE

LOCATION: *Niagara River, Ontario, Canada.*

VISITOR INFORMATION: *Niagara National Historic Sites, Box 787, Niagara-on-the-Lake, Ontario LOS 1JO, Canada.*

TELEPHONE: *905 468 4257*

DIRECTIONS: *Follow the road south from Toronto around Lake Ontario to Saint Catherines and on to Niagara-on-the-Lake.*

TOUR DISTANCE: *0.6 miles (1km).*

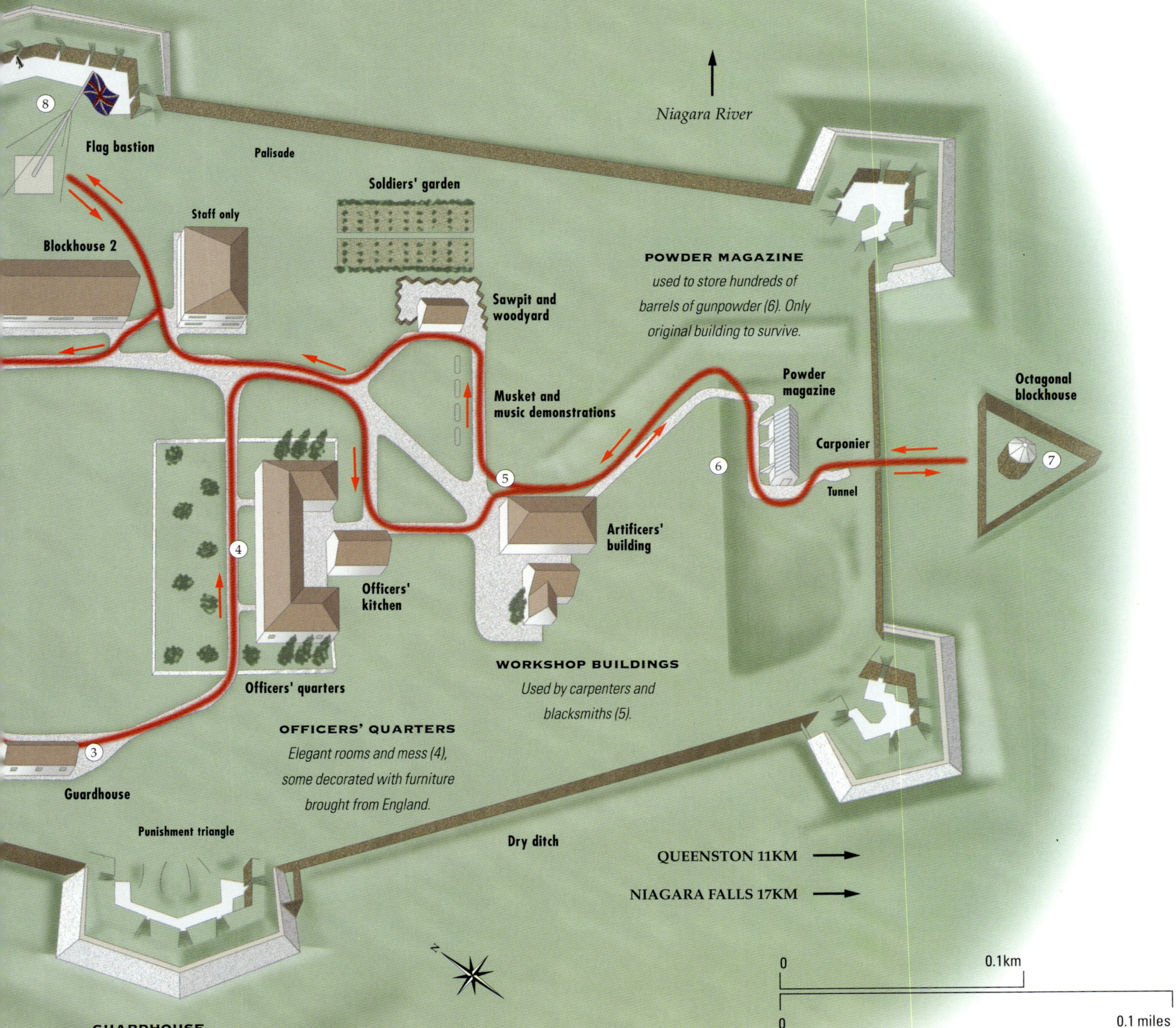

POWDER MAGAZINE

used to store hundreds of barrels of gunpowder (6). Only original building to survive.

WORKSHOP BUILDINGS

Used by carpenters and blacksmiths (5).

OFFICERS' QUARTERS

Elegant rooms and mess (4), some decorated with furniture brought from England.

GUARDHOUSE

Center of daily operations, all visitors had to report here (3). The punishment area is nearby.

FIRST BLOOD

Above ***The reconstructed Stone Bridge*** *at Bull Run River was the point of the first diversionary attack launched by the Union army.*

Left ***Brigadier General P.G. T. Beauregard,*** *commander of Confederate forces at the Battle of Bull Run. His personal presence on the battlefield helped stiffen Confederate resolve.*

The first battle of Bull Run was the first major battle of the American Civil War and has been called "one of the best planned but worst fought battles" of the conflict. The southern states were looking for first blood in 1861, having seceded earlier that year, and they were keen to defend their way of life. Jefferson Davis, the elected president of the Confederacy, was an ex-army man. Abraham Lincoln, newly elected president of the United States, had little military experience and ignored the advice of his senior military advisers. Two armies now gathered between the two capitals, intent on a major conflict.

COSTLY ERROR

Brevet Major General Irvin McDowell commanded 35,700 Union soldiers, whereas Major General Pierre G.T. Beauregard led 22,000 Confederates—the majority of both sides' soldiers being inexperienced volunteers. With his back to Washington, McDowell approached Beauregard, who was positioned near the railway junction of Manassas, Virginia. On July 18, a Confederate reconnaissance broke out into a clash and Union troops were smartly repulsed. This depressed Union morale and McDowell delayed further action to bring forward more supplies. It was a costly error. While the Union army postponed its attack, General Joseph E. Johnston rushed 12,000 reinforcements from Winchester to the Confederates by rail, thus roughly equalizing the forces.

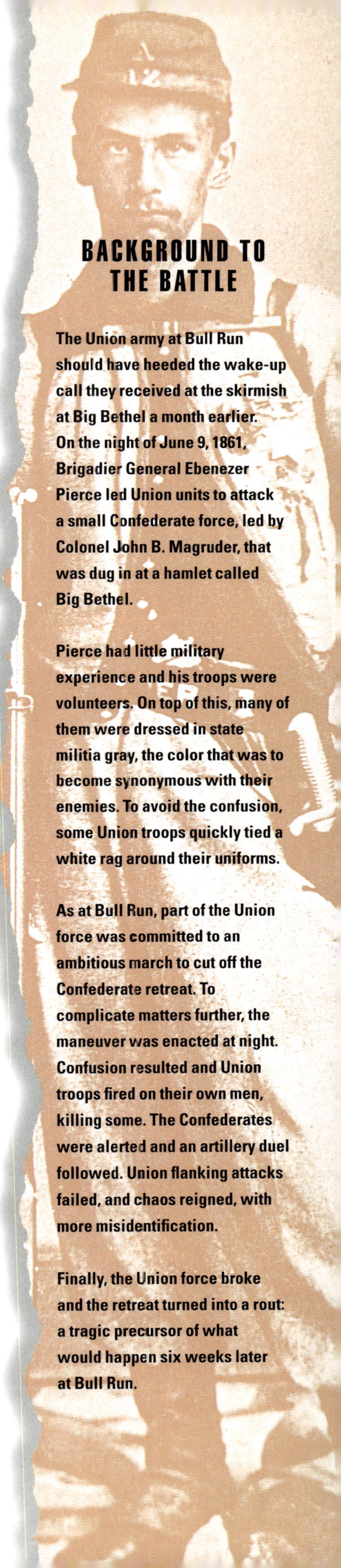

BACKGROUND TO THE BATTLE

The Union army at Bull Run should have heeded the wake-up call they received at the skirmish at Big Bethel a month earlier. On the night of June 9, 1861, Brigadier General Ebenezer Pierce led Union units to attack a small Confederate force, led by Colonel John B. Magruder, that was dug in at a hamlet called Big Bethel.

Pierce had little military experience and his troops were volunteers. On top of this, many of them were dressed in state militia gray, the color that was to become synonymous with their enemies. To avoid the confusion, some Union troops quickly tied a white rag around their uniforms.

As at Bull Run, part of the Union force was committed to an ambitious march to cut off the Confederate retreat. To complicate matters further, the maneuver was enacted at night. Confusion resulted and Union troops fired on their own men, killing some. The Confederates were alerted and an artillery duel followed. Union flanking attacks failed, and chaos reigned, with more misidentification.

Finally, the Union force broke and the retreat turned into a rout: a tragic precursor of what would happen six weeks later at Bull Run.

On Sunday July 21, early in the morning, McDowell began to maneuver his troops. At 5:30 A.M. a shot from a 30-pounder Parrott gun announced the attack. McDowell believed that the Confederate left flank was its weakest point and launched his main attack against it. Other Union attacks at the Stone Bridge over Bull Run and Blackburn's Ford were intended as diversions to screen this. The long, flanking march was challenging for the Union army volunteers and their inexperienced officers, but it still might have worked if it had not been spotted by a Confederate signal officer who warned the rest of his army. The Confederate army now moved troops away from the diversionary attack at the Stone Bridge to reinforce their position where the Warrenton Turnpike crossed the Manassas–Sudley Road.

RIGHT ***One of the many artillery pieces*** *to be seen on the battlefield of Bull Run in the Manassas National Park. Artillery duels played an important and devastating part in the battle. (Photo by Alec Hasenson.)*

BELOW ***Re-enactors recreate a firing line*** *of Confederate infantry, evoking some of the firepower present at Bull Run.*

Although discovered, the Union army pressed forward with its main attack and the Confederate line faltered under the pressure. Colonel Wade Hampton's Legion of 600 South Carolina soldiers at Robinson House helped cover the Confederate withdrawal, but even they were forced back with 121 casualties. It looked as though McDowell might well have been victorious but then, in the confusion, brigade commander Barnard E. Bee pointed his sword at Brigadier General Thomas J. Jackson's brigade on Henry Hill and shouted to the newly arrived 4th Alabama Infantry: "Form! Form! There stands Jackson like a stone wall! Rally behind the Virginians!" The legend of "Stonewall" Jackson was born and the crisis of the battle passed for the Confederates.

RUSH OF A GREAT RIVER

Confederate commanders Beauregard and Johnston rode onto the battlefield at midday and their presence stiffened the resolve of their troops. McDowell ordered his regular army gun batteries forward and a terrific cannon duel heralded the afternoon's fighting.

Union guns were protected by a splendid volunteer unit of red-shirted New York Irish firemen called the Fire Zouaves. Brigade commander Orlando Willcox describes the impact of enemy fire on these volunteer soldiers: "Just as the Zouaves came to the crest of the rising ground...the fire burst upon us from the whole pocket of woods which partially enclosed us...The weight of metal against us was as of ten shots to one, of every

BLIND PANIC

William Russell, correspondent for *The Times* of London at the Battle of Bull Run, was caught up in the Union retreat. At first he viewed it as an orderly withdrawal, but then panic gripped the soldiers around him, and the situation rapidly deteriorated:

"'The cavalry! Cavalry are coming!' rang through the crowd, and looking back to Centreville, I perceived coming down the hill, between me and the sky, a number of mounted men, who might, at a hasty glance, be taken for horsemen in the act of sabreing the fugitives. In reality, they were soldiers and civilians, with, I regret to say, some officers among them who were whipping and striking their horses with sticks or whatever else they could lay their hands on. I called out to the men who were frantic with terror beside me, 'They are not cavalry at all; they're your own men'—but they did not heed me. A fellow who was shouting out, 'Run! Run!' as loud as he could, beside me, seemed to take delight in creating alarm; and, as he was perfectly collected as far as I could judge, I said, 'What on earth are you running for? What are you afraid of?' He was in the roadside below me, and at once turning on me, and exclaiming, 'I'm not afraid of you,' presented his piece [pistol] and pulled the trigger so instantaneously, that, had it gone off, I could not have swerved from the ball."

Quoted from WILLIAM RUSSELL SPECIAL CORRESPONDENT *of* The Times, *edited by Roger Hudson (Folio Society, 1995).*

Battle of Bull Run, *showing the moment when Colonel J. E. B. Stuart's Confederate cavalry dispersed the Union infantry, including the colorfully attired Zouaves. (Lithograph by Kurz and Allison.)*

Right ***Private Francis E. Brownell,*** *volunteer member of the New York Fire Zouaves, first tasted combat at Bull Run. Volunteers to this unit came from the Irish firemen of New York. Their exotic uniforms were inspired by the Zouave fashion of the French Army who recruited similarly clad soldiers from North Africa.*

class of projectiles . . . the whole regiment was swept back as by a tornado."

Not even the reckless bravery of the Zouaves could save them from a sudden assault by Colonel J. E. B. Stuart and his 1st Virginia "Black Horse" Cavalry. Attack and counter-attack swept across the battlefield as both sides fought bitterly to maintain their gains. Further Confederate reinforcements now joined the battle and these late additions began to tell. A combined Confederate attack at 3:45 P.M., spearheaded by Colonel Jubal A. Early's brigade, proved the decisive factor—the Union line buckled.

Under concentrated artillery and musket fire, the thousands of Union volunteers had finally reached the end of their determination. Nerves broke and the men fell back across Sudley Ford and the Stone Bridge. During their retreat, a Confederate cannonball overturned a wagon on the suspension bridge over Cub Run, blocking the passage. This incident created panic among the withdrawing Union soldiers and turned their retreat into a rout all the way back to Washington. It was a humiliating end to a brave fight by both sides, but McDowell's repeated attempts at rallying his men failed. They had simply had enough. The roar of their flight, wrote *The Times*' correspondent, was like the rush of a great river.

It was a shocking result for the North and profoundly effected their morale. In the South, elation encouraged the Confederates to think that the war was over. Lincoln responded with grim resolution and a strategy determined not to let Washington fall to the rebels. The Confederates in their turn lost the advantage of the victory by not pursuing the collapsed army and were overconfident in the abilities of their men. Total casualties were 2,896 for the Union army and 1,982 for the Confederates.

BULL RUN

THE FIRST BATTLE OF BULL RUN is named by Northerners after the river that runs through the battlefield, but the conflict is also known to Southerners as the first Battle of Manassas—from the railway junction nearby that proved crucial in bringing up Confederate reinforcements. Two Civil War battles were fought over this land, the latter one taking place in August 1862, seeing General Robert E. Lee and Major General John Pope clash in a second victory for the Confederates.

The battleground today is a well-preserved national battlefield park with a visitor center on Henry Hill. It was here that the Confederate forces finally rallied against the Union assault, most famously under "Stonewall" Jackson who earned his nickname here. The original Henry House was completely destroyed in battle, with its owner, Mrs. Judith Henry, being killed by artillery fire during the first Bull Run. A replica house has since been built on the site and Mrs. Henry's grave lies in its yard. Nearby is one of the earliest memorials raised to commemorate the Civil War—the Union Monument—a stone pyramid built to honor the memory of dead comrades.

Brigadier General Thomas Jonathan "Stonewall" Jackson *won his famous nickname at the Battle of Bull Run as his troops held their position against intense Union attacks. (Portrait by J. A. Elder.)*

Robinson House was owned by a "free Negro" called James Robinson and received little battle damage until it was ransacked by Union soldiers, for which he received compensation of $1,249.

The Stone Bridge was the scene of the first fighting at Bull Run and was one of the main avenues for the final Union retreat. Although destroyed in the fighting, it has since been rebuilt. Sudley Church marks the ford across which McDowell's Union army executed its ambitious flanking maneuver. The church was used as a Union hospital.

PLAN OF BATTLE

A predawn diversionary attack at the Stone Bridge began the battle, but Union commander McDowell's main attack was a long, flanking maneuver that crossed Sudley Ford to strike at the Confederate left wing. The Confederates shifted their main body of men away from Bull Run to meet this assault on Matthews Hill and then Henry Hill, where they stood their ground and launched counterattacks that finally shattered Union determination.

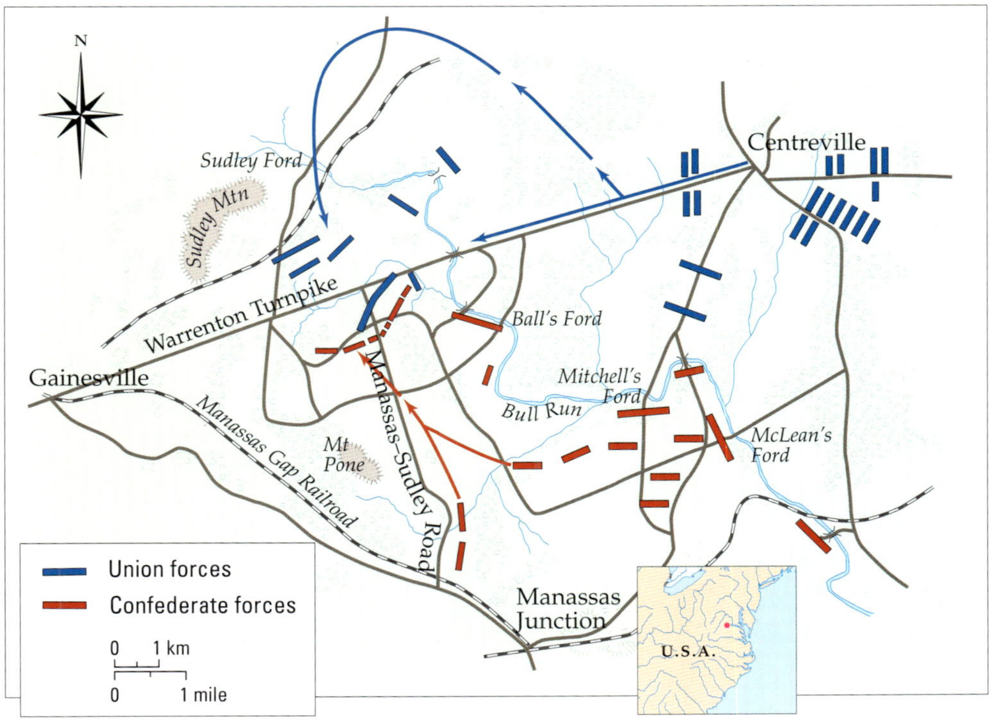

BULL RUN

The Manassas National Battlefield Park preserves the battlefield across which both battles of Bull Run were fought. All the major locations of combat are clearly marked, and it makes an easy day-trip from Washington D.C.

SUDLEY CHURCH

McDowell's Union army crossed the ford nearby Sudley Church (7) to begin their main flanking attack on the Confederate army. The church was used as a hospital during the battle.

Left *The Stone House (4) at Manassas National Park* *is the best-preserved building from the first Battle of Bull Run. It served as a hospital for the soldiers during the battle, and shells can still be seen embedded in its walls. Immediately after the war, it served as an inn. (Photo by Alec Hasenson.)*

Left *The Bull Run Monument near Henry House* *was erected in 1865 in memory of the Union troops who died at the first Battle of Bull Run. It was one of the earliest memorials to be built after the Civil War. (Photo by Alec Hasenson.)*

RIGHT *Ruins of the Stone Bridge (6)* *at Bull Run River, over which Union troops retreated back to Washington D.C.*

GETTING THERE

LOCATION: *Manassas, Virginia, U.S.A.*

VISITOR INFORMATION: *Manassas National Battlefield Park, 12521 Lee Highway, Manassas, VA 20109*

TELEPHONE: *703 361 1339*

DIRECTION: *Park is situated in Prince William County, 26 miles (39km) southwest of Washington D.C. on State Route 234.*

TOUR DISTANCE: *13 miles (21km).*

STONE HOUSE

Located on Matthews Hill is the Stone House (4) from where the Confederates first attempted to halt the Union main assault.

STONE BRIDGE

The Stone Bridge (6) was the scene of the first diversionary Union attack, and then served as one of the exit points over Bull Run River for the retreating Union army. The road leads on to Cub Run Bridge where panic gripped the Union army.

ROBINSON HOUSE

Stiff Confederate resistance at Robinson House (3) led by Hampton's Legion was eventually forced back by the Union army.

HENRY HILL

Henry Hill (12) was the center of Confederate resistance to Union attacks and where "Stonewall" Jackson won his nickname. Many memorials and statues are here, plus the visitor center. Henry House has been rebuilt nearby.

RIGHT *The monument to General Jackson* *stands near the Visitor Center (1) on Henry Hill. General Jackson earned his nickname "Stonewall" at the first Battle of Bull Run. Its Art Deco exaggeration of the unprepossessing hero's physique has earned it the local nickname of "Stonewall on steroids."*

KEY TO THE SOUTH

ABOVE *Heavy 17,000-pound mortars* *were used by the Union army in previous attacks on Vicksburg, hurling 200-pound shells into the city to devastating effect, but without breaking the defenses around the city.*

LEFT *Union forces attempt to storm* *the defenses of Vicksburg, but such assaults achieved little, and the Union army had to settle down to await the outcome of their siege. (Painting by H. Charles McBarron.)*

"VICKSBURG IS THE KEY," proclaimed President Abraham Lincoln. "The war can never be brought to a close until the key is in our pocket." Confederate President Jefferson Davis called Vicksburg "the nailhead that held the South's two halves together." Perched high on bluffs overlooking the Mississippi, it commanded the river as well as being a vital railway junction linking the eastern and western states of the Confederacy. But it was a hard nut to crack. Its west side was protected by the river; its east side was surrounded by a jungle-like swamp. To this was added formidable fortifications, including trenches and redoubts. Union ships dominated the river, but they could not pass under the guns of Vicksburg. Everything pointed at its capture, but the Union army had already failed to take it six times in 1862 and 1863. Major General Ulysses S. Grant had been in charge of many of these attempts and his continued failure was beginning to draw criticism. Lincoln, however, stood by him and his faith was to be rewarded.

HE CAN FIGHT

Ulysses S. Grant was an unlikely soldier, performing poorly at West Point and resigning his commission to become a farmer. When the Civil War came, he volunteered, but was not promoted immediately to high rank. It was only when he demonstrated his aggression and skill in command that he became a general. His personal faults of being profane and drinking to excess mattered little to Lincoln, who commented: "I need that man; he can fight." Vicksburg was to be his greatest test.

BACKGROUND TO BATTLE

Previous assaults on Vicksburg give some idea of what a difficult target it was for Grant.

In April 1862, Captain David G. Farragut arrived at Vicksburg with his squadron, including eight steam sloops and corvettes, a twenty-ship mortar flotilla, and nine gunboats. Fresh from victory at New Orleans, he was full of optimism but suffered badly from the artillery situated high on the bluffs and was discouraged from any further assault.

In December 1862, Grant moved on the city from the north, with Sherman commanding a fleet on the river while he attacked from the land. Two Confederate cavalry raids countered Grant's advance, while Sherman was defeated at Chickasaw Bluffs after three days of fighting.

In early 1863 Grant oversaw four more attempted assaults on Vicksburg. Two of these involved over-ambitious canal plans, while the third plan—to approach through the Yazoo Delta with gunboats and transport ships—was halted by a Confederate strongpoint at Greenwood.

Finally, in March 1863, Rear Admiral Porter personally led a flotilla through Steel's Bayou, but it became bogged down in the jungle-like environment and had to be rescued by Grant.

ABOVE ***A section of rifle pits*** *constructed for Union sharpshooters during the siege of Vicksburg. Union snipers helped keep the heads of Confederate soldiers down, thus enabling the Union army to push forward its siegeworks. (Contemporary engraving.)*

Grant viewed the assault on Vicksburg as a combined services operation. Rear Admiral David D. Porter took his Mississippi fleet down the river past the guns of Vicksburg and met Grant at Hard Times Landing, where he assembled two corps of Union troops. Major General William T. Sherman provided a diversionary force nearer Vicksburg. Grant now crossed the Mississippi and defeated a Confederate force at Port Gibson on May 1. It was a risky move, as he was now without his supply line along the Mississippi, but he plunged into enemy territory, determined to live off the land. Over the next seventeen days, Grant outmaneuvered the Confederates and defeated them piecemeal.

On May 19 and 22 Grant arrived outside Vicksburg and attempted to take it by assault, but failed. "I now determined upon a regular siege," he recalled, "to 'outcamp the enemy,' as it were, and to incur no more losses. The experience of May 22 convinced officers and men that this was best, and they went to work on the defenses and approaches. With the navy holding the river, the investment of Vicksburg was complete. As long as we could hold our position the enemy was limited in supplies of food, men, and munitions of war to what they had on hand. These could not last always."

Pick and spade took over from musket and sword, and Union soldiers dug a complex of trenches and emplacements, reinforced with sandbags and logs. Union sharpshooters kept the defenders' heads down. "We had no siege guns except six thirty-two pounders," wrote Grant. "Admiral Porter, however, supplied us with a battery of navy guns of large caliber, and with these, and the field artillery used in the campaign, the siege began." Some mortars were even constructed out of hollowed-out logs bound with iron bands, which could then fire six- or twelve-pound shells. Grant, a passionate abolitionist, noted that much of the trench digging work was carried out "by negroes who came within our lines and who were paid for their work."

SIEGE LIFE

Ammunition began running low inside Vicksburg, preventing the Confederate soldiers from firing too frequently at their besiegers. There were not as many troops to rotate

Left ***Heavy mortars*** *used by the Union army during siege warfare.*

front-line duty as there were among the Union army, making the siege particularly grueling for men who had to be on guard for attack all day and night. Nearly 3,500 Confederates were killed or wounded during the siege.

Whereas the Union army was well provided with food, the Confederates had to survive on increasingly low and improvised rations. Coffee was brewed using sweet potatoes, blackberry leaves, and sassafras. For flour there was ground peas and corn meal. One soldier complained that when it was baked "It made a nauseous composition, as the cornmeal cooked in half the time the peas meal did, so the stuff was half raw...It had the properties of india rubber and was worse than leather to digest." Mules began to be slaughtered for their meat.

HELLO YANK

Although the siege of Vicksburg was bitterly fought by both sides, there were moments when the soldiers could relax and communicate with each other over the siegeworks. One anonymous Union soldier remembers a typical exchange between both sides:

"In the evening when everything had stopped for the day, some of our men or some of the Johnnies [Confederates] would yell, 'Hello Johnnie' or 'Hello Yank.' 'How did you enjoy the day?' The other would say 'Fine'; then someone would say, 'Johnnie, how do you like mule meat?' and they answer 'Fine'; then 'How do you like beef dried on the bone?' to which they would reply 'Not so well; it is too close to the bone to be good.' Then someone would say, 'Come over and we will give you some sow belly to fry it in . . .' So you see how soon those on both sides forgot their troubles when night came, but in the morning about daylight, when the business of the day was about to open, we would say, 'Watch out, Johnnie, and hunt your hole,' and things were on in earnest for the day."

Quoted in VICKSBURG *by William C. Everhart, (Washington D.C., 1954).*

Right ***This fine statue of a Union soldier*** *is one of many memorials to be seen at the Vicksburg National Park. (Photo by Alec Hasenson.)*

ABOVE *Remains of the Union trench of Logan's Division,* *now part of the Vicksburg National Park. (Photo by Alec Hasenson.)*

Life for civilians inside Vicksburg was just as bleak. Under constant shellfire, many civilians occupied caves dug in the hills of the city. Despite the bombardment and lack of food, however, some normalcy continued, with the Vicksburg newspaper still being printed, although on wallpaper. Women assisted as nurses, looking after the thousands of Confederate sick and wounded. Lighter moments occurred when Northern soldiers on picket duty swapped coffee for Southern tobacco with the besieged.

Several more attempts were made to attack Vicksburg, including a ship-borne assault, which led to the sinking of the gunboat *Cincinnati*, and the exploding of a mine under the redan (a fortification of two parapets at a salient angle) of the 3rd Louisiana. It created a huge crater, but the Confederates already knew of it and had retired to another line of defense. Any chance of relief coming for the Confederates was dashed by the defeat of an attack at Miliken's Bend by two regiments of freed slaves. It was the first major action by black troops in the Civil War.

Eventually, after forty-seven days of bombardment and starvation, Lieutenant General John C. Pemberton, commander of Vicksburg, surrendered the city to Grant on July 4, 1863. It was a tremendous victory for Grant and the North, as it cut the Confederacy in half and hastened the end of the war. But the mood among the Confederates was bitter, and Independence Day was not celebrated in Vicksburg for many years.

BELOW *Siege of Vicksburg,* *showing Union siegeworks around Confederate bastion in the background, on the bank of the Mississippi River. (Lithograph by Kurz and Allison.)*

FORTIFICATIONS OF VICKSBURG

A LARGE SECTION OF THE Confederate fortifications and Union siegeworks around Vicksburg have been preserved as a National Military Park. Trench lines and redoubts are covered in grass but are still visible, some reconstructions of the timber breastworks can be viewed near the Visitor Center, artillery pieces are scattered all over the battlefield, and there are a remarkable 1,200 monuments and markers around the battlefield park. There are many more trees now than there would have been at the time; during the siege, the area would have been bleak with many trees cut down to strengthen the trenches and siegeworks.

***A military postman on horseback** delivers news of the siege to Confederate refugees camped near Vicksburg. (Contemporary engraving.)*

The action following the blowing up of a mine can be clearly traced at the park. A Union mine was exploded under the 3rd Louisiana redan, a key Confederate strongpoint. The attack was launched by the 45th Illinois Infantry from their headquarters at Shirley House, which has been restored. They then advanced along Logan's Approach, a trench leading toward the fortifications that you can still walk along, past the Illinois Memorial. The explosion left a crater twelve feet deep and forty feet wide. Unfortunately for the Union troops, the attack was not successful, as the Confederates had already withdrawn from the redan and they poured intense fire into the attacking Union troops, including rolling short-fuse shells down into the crater on the trapped men.

Grant's headquarters were located in the northeastern part of the park, and are marked by an impressive statue of the general on horseback. Grant's rival, Pemberton, is commemorated with a statue at the southern end of the park. At the northwest end of the park, visitors can see a section of the Yazoo Canal, evocative of the waterlogged land that defeated Union attempts so many times.

PLAN OF BATTLE

Grant tried and failed several times to command the waterlogged land around Vicksburg with amphibious assaults and the use of military supply canals. Finally, in April 1863, he began his successful campaign at Hard Times Landing, where he crossed his troops in the boats that survived the gun batteries in the city. A series of victories against overwhelming Confederate numbers enabled Grant to secure the surrounding area and then lay siege to Vicksburg.

VICKSBURG

THE VICKSBURG NATIONAL MILITARY PARK forms an arc behind the business area of Vicksburg. Two main roads provide access to the park and trace the lines of battle. Union Avenue parallels the Union siege line, and Confederate Avenue parallels the Confederate defensive perimeter. Iron tablets throughout the park locate principal combat areas.

ABOVE ***Vicksburg National Cemetery*** *was established in 1866 to reinter the remains of nearly 17,000 Union soldiers who were given only temporary burial during the Civil War. (Photo by Alec Hasenson.)*

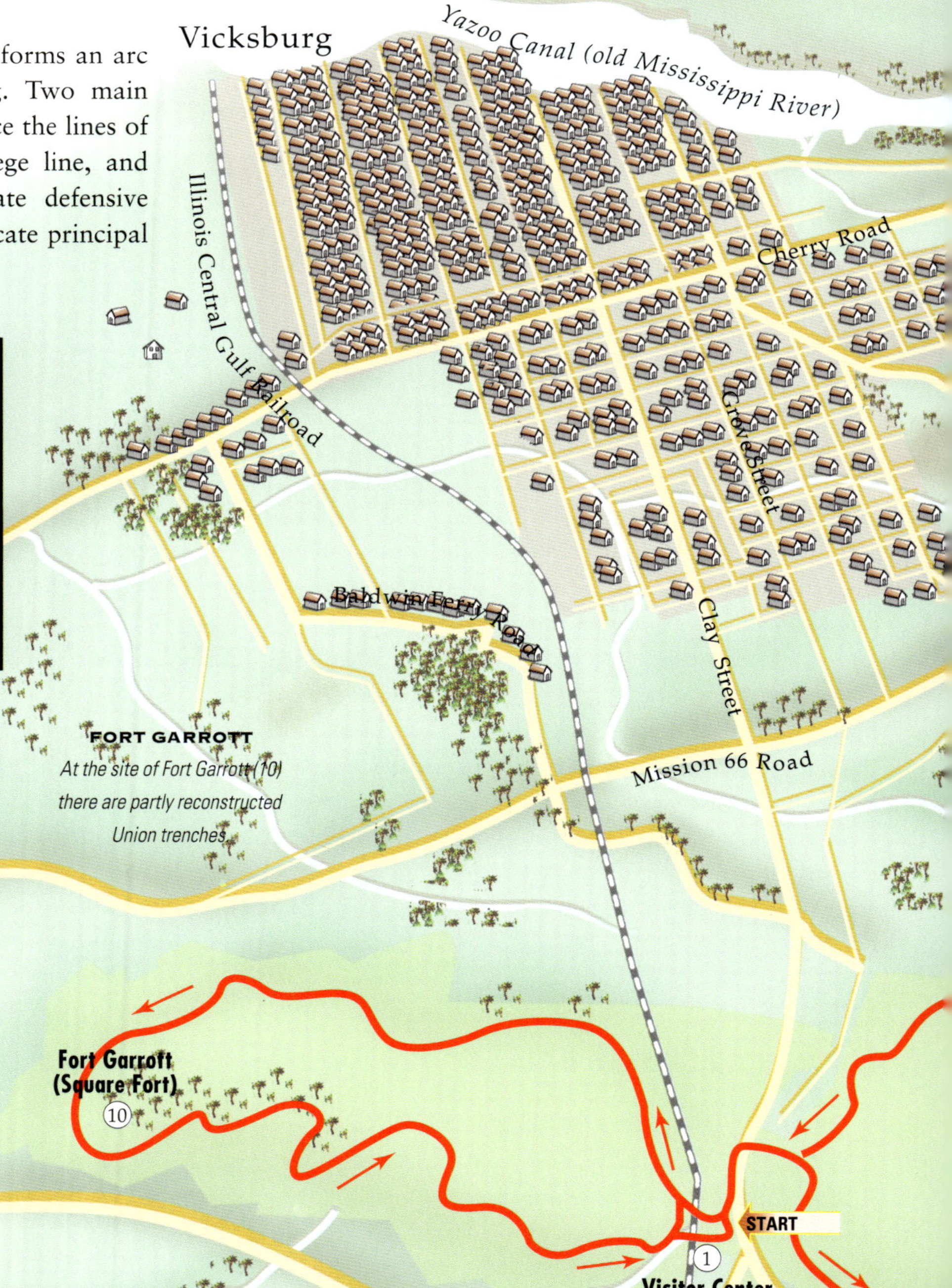

FORT GARROTT

At the site of Fort Garrott (10) there are partly reconstructed Union trenches.

VISITOR CENTER

A movie reconstructing the events of the siege can be watched at the Visitor Center (1).

GETTING THERE

LOCATION: *Vicksburg, Mississippi.*

VISITOR INFORMATION: *Superintendent, Vicksburg National Military Park, 3201 Clay Street, Vicksburg, MS 39180. Vicksburg Convention and Visitors Bureau, P.O. Box 110, Vicksburg, MS 39181.*

TELEPHONE: *Vicksburg Visitors Bureau 1-800-221-3536*

DIRECTIONS: *The Park forms a semicircle around the east side of Vicksburg, and is located at the intersection of US 80 and 61, midway between Memphis and New Orleans.*

TOUR DISTANCE: *14 miles (22km).*

LEFT ***Union cannons stand in the remains of a trench at Vicksburg.*** *The Napoleon 12-pounder model 1857 was the most used cannon at the siege of Vicksburg, its smoothbore barrel firing a variety of shot, including shell and canister, over an effective range of just under a mile. In the background is the monument to the Michigan soldiers that fought in the campaign. (Photo by Alec Hasenson.)*

Above ***The remains of U.S.S.*** **Cairo,** *a Union ironclad gunboat sunk by a mine in the Yazoo Delta in 1862. Raised in 1964, she is now the centerpiece of a museum (7) in the Vicksburg National Park. Gunboats such as this played a key role in the battle for control of the great rivers during the Civil War. (Photo by Alec Hasenson.)*

Right, ***Reconstructed log palisade,*** *typical of the defenses built by both sides during the siege of Vicksburg. (Photo by Alec Hasenson.)*

THE BLOODY CREEK

ABOVE *Monument to the German American 9th Ohio Infantry* *who advanced along La Fayette Road to repulse a Confederate assault threatening Thomas' battle line. (Photo by Alec Hasenson.)*

LEFT *Union soldiers of the 6th Maine Infantry Regiment* *on parade. Uniforms were one of the first casualties of war, as Major Connolly at Chickamauga wrote to his wife: "If my dear mother could see me, she would laugh first and then cry to see me looking so much like a beggar man; my coat is out at the elbows and all the lining torn out . . . and my hat the very picture of misery and dilapidation . . . "*

WITH THE COMMANDER IN CHIEF of Union forces, Major General Ulysses S. Grant, outside Vicksburg, the Confederacy was beginning to feel the pressure of Union strategy. On July 4, 1863, the Confederate strongpoint fell and, almost simultaneously, Confederate General Robert E. Lee was dealt a severe defeat at Gettysburg. The situation looked grim for the South, and Union Major General William S. Rosecrans took advantage of it. In late summer, he pushed across the Tennessee River and threatened Confederate General Braxton Bragg's line of communication to Atlanta, forcing the Confederates to abandon Chattanooga and retreat into Georgia. Southern President Jefferson Davis could see Bragg needed support and rushed him reinforcements by rail, bringing Bragg's army up to a strength of 70,000, slightly more than that of his opponent, and enabling Bragg to turn on his pursuer.

BACKGROUND TO BATTLE

With recent major victories at Vicksburg and Gettysburg, the mood among Rosecrans' Union troops was optimistic.

Major James Austin Connolly, a member of Rosecrans' army, reported a vital insight into the contrasting Confederate morale two days before the Battle of Chickamauga: "We captured a large rebel mail . . . and I read probably 200 of the letters, . . . and such a gloomy, despondent bunch of manuscript, relating to the Southern Confederacy, I never dreamed of."

Connolly later writes that the Confederates "come swarming into our lines daily." In the wake of this collapse in Confederate morale, he suggests that the best military strategy is not to fight a major battle, but to let desertion slowly drain away forces from the South. That said, he admits, "Two such hostile armies can't lie so close to each other many days without breeding trouble."

The trouble to follow was the Battle of Chickamauga where Confederate troops threw off their despondency and fought with a spirit undimmed by past failures in a classic example of how troops can pull victory from defeat.

CONFRONTATION

On September 18, Bragg's Confederates advanced across Chickamauga Creek and confronted Rosecrans' army. Union cavalry delayed the Southern troops long enough for Rosecrans to prepare his men. The following day, both armies continued their maneuvering, sliding into combat in the hilly woodlands between Chickamauga Creek and Missionary Ridge. Rosecrans' goal was to maintain control of La Fayette Road, which gave him access to his line of communication to Chattanooga. Bragg just wanted to destroy the enemy. Both sides fought hard. At one point, Union troops gained the advantage, then a section of their line gave way and Confederates poured through, only to be met by Union reinforcements. By the end of the day, both sides were worn out with little to show for their efforts. As the sun set, a Confederate assault was made but this ended with many dead and little achieved.

ABOVE *Major General William S. Rosecrans,* *commander of Union forces at Chickamauga, plucked defeat from the jaws of victory.*

RIGHT *Union soldier with family in camp.* *A few wives and children could travel with their husbands on campaign, but they frequently had to work hard and provide services for other soldiers in the camp, including washing and cooking. (Photograph by Mathew Brady.)*

During the night, Rosecrans further secured his battle line on his left flank with log breastworks and reinforcements. His position was roughly parallel to La Fayette Road. Bragg opened the day's fighting by sending his right wing under Lieutenant General Leonidas Polk against Rosecrans' well-defended left flank under the command of Major General George H. Thomas. It was a predictable disaster. Polk's brave men were slaughtered. The Confederates attacked "with a fury . . ." wrote Union

DESPERATE COURAGE

The stand of Thomas and his Union troops at Chickamauga was truly heroic, resisting countless brave and bold assaults by the Confederate army. Brigadier General John Beatty later paid homage to the extraordinary Union resistance:

"Men fought and struggled and clung to that ridge with an obstinate persistence, desperate courage, unsurpassed, I believe, on any field. I robbed the dead of cartridges and distributed them to the men; and once when, after a desperate struggle, our troops were driven from the crest and the enemy's flag waved above it, the men were rallied, and I rode up the hill with them, waving my hat and shouting like a madman. Thus we charged, and the enemy only saved his colors by throwing them down the hill. However much we may say of those who held command, justice compels the acknowledgment that no officer exhibited more courage on that occasion than the humblest private in the ranks."

Quoted in CHICKAMAUGA *by Steven E. Woodworth (University of Nebraska Press, 1999).*

Height of the Battle of Chickamauga *showing the intense firefights between Union and Confederate troops. (Lithograph by Kurz and Allison.)*

Brigadier General William B. Hazen. "The repulse was equally terrific and final...The value of this simple breastwork will be understood..."

Although fatal for the men involved, Polk's assault had the effect of encouraging the Union center to move leftward to support the flank under attack. This left a gap in the Union line between Viniard and Brotherton houses to be exploited by Confederate Lieutenant General James Longstreet.

ROCK OF CHICKAMAUGA

Longstreet's impact was devastating. Union artillery and infantry under Major General Philip H. Sheridan fought bitterly, but the overall effect was the collapse of the Union center and right. "The sight was truly appalling," recalled a member of the 36th Illinois. "The ground was covered with dry grass and old logs which the bursting shells had set on fire. A thick cloud of smoke had risen about as high as our heads...Under this we could see, ...just as far as the eye could reach, moving masses of men hurrying toward us." Panic tore through the Northern ranks and a portion of the army fled all the way back to Chattanooga, including Rosecrans himself. Rosecrans considered going back to organize a last-ditch defense, but his chief of staff, Major General James A. Garfield, convinced him to ride on to Chattanooga instead, while Garfield checked on Thomas' situation—this decision cost Rosecrans his command and his career.

Ironically, the Union left wing under Thomas, which had been the cause of the debacle elsewhere, was now reinforced and held firm. As the senior officer left on the field, Thomas took control of all Union forces and, with the addition of some reinforcements, held on to his position all day, despite Longstreet's determination for victory.

Union tactics on the ground helped their troops last the long day, despite both sides being exhausted. Union troops had the advantage of defense, whereas the Confederates had to run up and down exposed on the hills of the terrain. Union soldiers of Harker's brigade would lie down between assaults and then rise in lines to deliver their volleys, reloading and sheltering as others fired in turn. Thomas' physical presence, sitting stolidly among the noise and confusion, was also fundamental to the morale of the Union soldiers.

By holding on, Thomas earned the nickname of "Rock of Chickamauga." By nightfall, however, Rosecrans sent orders for Thomas to withdraw and he retreated in good order in the darkness, ending the battle. The Confederates had won a painful victory. "At sunset," recalled a soldier of the 20th Tennessee, "everyone seemed wild with joy, from generals down to privates, all joined in the exultant cheer that rang over the bloodstained field." "It was the ugliest sound that any mortal ever heard," remembered a Union soldier. Confederate casualties outnumbered those of the Union army, 18,472 to 16,170. Exhausted, Bragg made no effort to pursue Rosecrans. Union commander Grant, having to relieve Rosecrans from a siege at Chattanooga, later replaced Rosecrans with Thomas.

Above *Unknown Confederate soldier* *posing with a rifle and shotgun in a photographer's studio.*

CHICKAMAUGA

General Braxton Bragg, overall commander of Confederate troops at Chickamauga.

ALTHOUGH WELL PRESERVED as a National Park, there are some aspects of the battlefield at Chickamauga that have changed over the years. For one, it is more thickly wooded today than in 1863 when battlefield visibility would have been greater. The heart of the battlefield, the frontline of Major General Thomas' position on the Union left flank, was marked at the time by a semicircular line of fieldworks, but is now Battle Line Road. La Fayette Road, running north to south through the park, is at the center of the battlefield and parallels the Union lines, now lined by monuments.

Chickamauga National Park is full of excellent monuments, many of them representing the places where individual units fought and fell. The monument to the 9th Ohio Infantry recalls their part in Colonel Ferdinand Van Derveer's brigade, which marched out of Kelly Field to turn along La Fayette Road and halt a Confederate assault on the far left of Thomas' battle line. They then counterattacked and forced the Confederates back, a brilliant display of what veteran soldiers could achieve under experienced officers. The 9th Ohio Regiment had a reputation for daring bayonet charges which they displayed at Chickamauga, compelling other Union units to join them in throwing back the Confederates.

Snodgrass Hill is where Thomas earned the nickname of "Rock of Chickamauga." A monument stands nearby, surmounted by the statue of a tiger to represent Opdycke's Tigers, the 125th Ohio commanded by Colonel Emerson Opdycke who was told by Thomas to hold the position. Opdycke replied: "We will hold this ground or go to Heaven from it." As good as his word, his unit held it until told to retire, losing 105 men out of 314.

PLAN OF BATTLE

The first day of fighting at Chickamauga was indecisive. During the night, the Union army had the good sense to further protect its position by digging fieldworks. These proved crucial when Polk opened the Confederate assault on the second day with an attack against the Union left commanded by Thomas. Rosecrans' great error was to send troops in his center to reinforce this position. Confederate Longstreet then broke through the weakened center and the Union army largely collapsed, except for Thomas' reinforced left wing which remained solidly in the battle until nightfall when ordered to retreat.

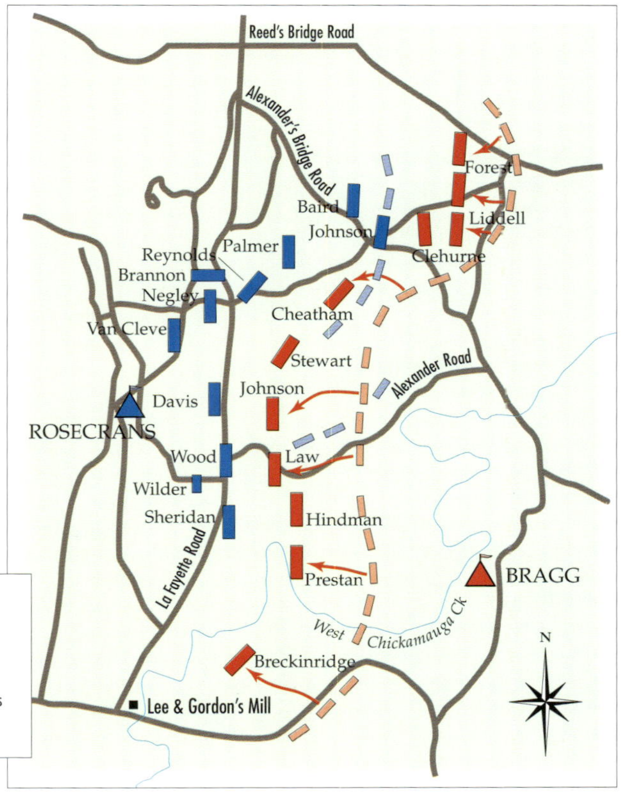

CHICKAMAUGA

CHICKAMAUGA NATIONAL BATTLEFIELD PARK is a short drive south from Chattanooga and is well preserved, with an excellent Visitor Center Museum and a signposted tour of the battlefield.

GETTING THERE

LOCATION: *Three miles (5km) north of Chickamauga Creek, Georgia.*

VISITOR INFORMATION: *Chickamauga National Military Park, P. O. Box 2128, Fort Oglethorpe, GA 30742.*

TELEPHONE: *706 866 9241*

DIRECTIONS: *15 miles (24km) south from Chattanooga, located off U.S. Highway 27.*

TOUR DISTANCE: *7 miles (11km).*

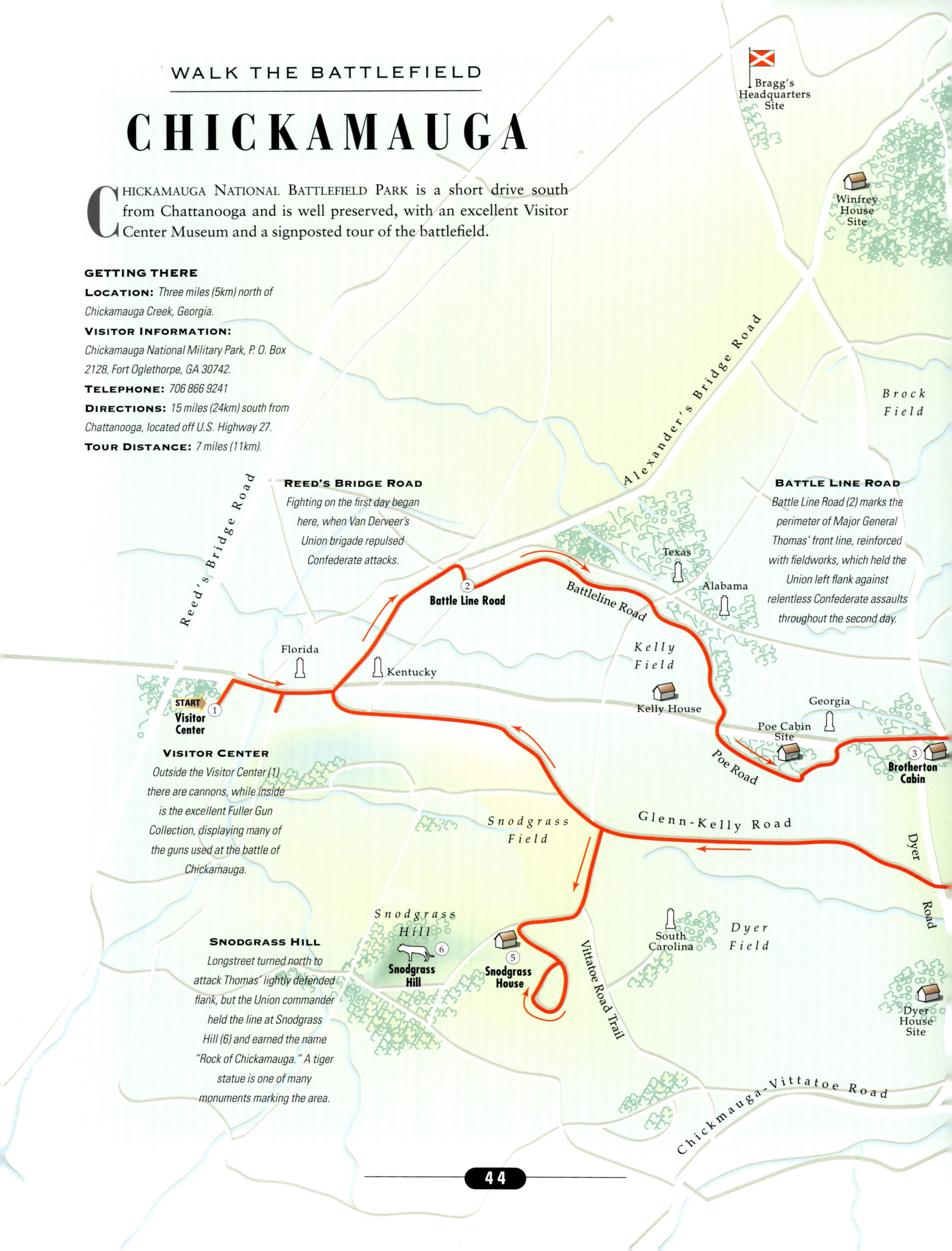

REED'S BRIDGE ROAD

Fighting on the first day began here, when Van Derveer's Union brigade repulsed Confederate attacks.

BATTLE LINE ROAD

Battle Line Road (2) marks the perimeter of Major General Thomas' front line, reinforced with fieldworks, which held the Union left flank against relentless Confederate assaults throughout the second day.

VISITOR CENTER

Outside the Visitor Center (1) there are cannons, while inside is the excellent Fuller Gun Collection, displaying many of the guns used at the battle of Chickamauga.

SNODGRASS HILL

Longstreet turned north to attack Thomas' lightly defended flank, but the Union commander held the line at Snodgrass Hill (6) and earned the name "Rock of Chickamauga." A tiger statue is one of many monuments marking the area.

Above *A cannonball monument* *marks the site where one of eight brigade commanders fell during the Battle of Chickamauga. (Photo by Alec Hasenson.)*

Right *The Union statue at Chickamauga* *reflects Northern pride at the resolute stand made by Major General Thomas and his men, even though the battle was a victory for the Confederates. (Photo by Alec Hasenson.)*

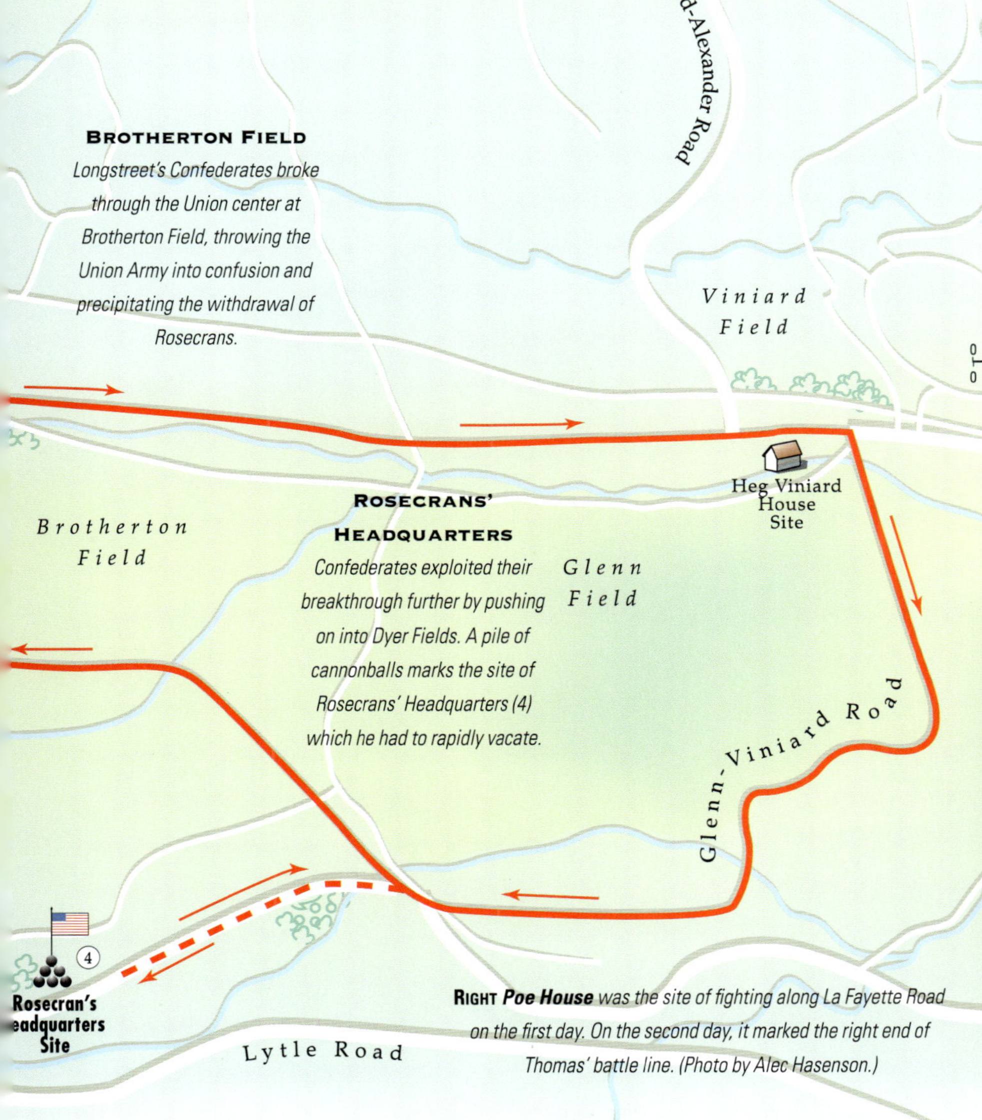

Brotherton Field

Longstreet's Confederates broke through the Union center at Brotherton Field, throwing the Union Army into confusion and precipitating the withdrawal of Rosecrans.

Rosecrans' Headquarters

Confederates exploited their breakthrough further by pushing on into Dyer Fields. A pile of cannonballs marks the site of Rosecrans' Headquarters (4) which he had to rapidly vacate.

Right *Poe House* *was the site of fighting along La Fayette Road on the first day. On the second day, it marked the right end of Thomas' battle line. (Photo by Alec Hasenson.)*

CUSTER'S LAST STAND

Above ***The monument on Custer Hill,*** *erected in 1881, lists the names of all the soldiers who died in the Battle of Little Bighorn.*

Left ***George Armstrong Custer,*** *commander of the 7th U.S. Cavalry at Little Bighorn and author, many think, of his own destruction. (Photo by Mathew Brady.)*

The Battle of Little Bighorn is perhaps the most famous conflict between Native Americans and the U.S. government. It has been the subject of endless books and numerous movies. Its impact on the popular imagination at the time was similar to that of the defeat at Isandlwana in southern Africa in which a group of Victorian soldiers was also wiped out by native warriors. It showed that even at a time when Westerners thought they were the superior messengers of civilization, they were vulnerable to bitter counterattacks by more primitive peoples defending their ways of life. At the heart of this drama in Montana was the figure of Lieutenant Colonel George Armstrong Custer.

YELLOW HAIR

Custer has been described as a paradoxical combination of virtue and vice. "A strict disciplinarian with those he commanded," says American historian Peter Newark, "Custer himself was often insubordinate and disobedient to his superiors and was once court-martialed and suspended from rank and command for a year. He neither smoked, drank liquor, nor used bad language, but he was an inveterate gambler." He fought with

BACKGROUND TO BATTLE

The clashes between the settlers of the American West and the Native Americans between 1865 and 1890 are known as the Indian Wars. Much of the fighting took the form of guerrilla raids in which Indians would pillage and kill settlers, only to be pursued by the U.S. army who would attempt to engage them in battle.

War began in Montana as settlers searched for gold and invaded the territory of the Sioux. Chief Red Cloud and his allies struck back successfully and won the Treaty of Fort Laramie in 1868. The U.S. army withdrew its garrisons from forts along the Bozeman Trail that led into Indian territory.

Two more wars followed when the Modoc left their reservation in Oregon to return to their land in California. This struggle was won by the U.S. army in 1873, and the Modoc leaders were hanged.

On the Southern Plains in 1874, the Kiowa and Comanche fought against some 3,000 U.S. soldiers. The army destroyed the Indians' winter camp, forcing the Indians to surrender.

Conflict next broke out on the Northern Plains when the Sioux and Cheyenne retaliated against invasion by gold miners. This was the Battle of Little Bighorn, and was the Indians' greatest victory against the U.S. army.

distinction in the American Civil War as a cavalry officer and was promoted to Major General, but after the war the army was reorganized and he was reassigned as Lieutenant Colonel to the newly formed 7th U.S. Cavalry. Native Americans had their own name for him, Yellow Hair, after his blond hair that he wore long in the frontier fashion.

In 1868, Custer led the 7th Cavalry to success in the Battle of the Washita, a dawn assault on a Cheyenne village. In 1874, he led an exploratory expedition through the Black Hills of South Dakota, which resulted in the discovery of gold, but this land was part of the Great Sioux reservation declared in 1868. Despite the government trying to protect the rights of the Sioux, gold hunters entered the land and violated the treaty. The government tried to buy the land for six million dollars but the Sioux refused to sell and the tension broke out into fighting in 1876.

Crazy Horse, a warrior of the Oglala Sioux, was one of the most prominent Indians to face Custer in Montana. He had already tasted victory over the U.S. army at the Fetterman massacre in 1866 and then clashed with Brigadier General George Crook ten years later. He led a combined force of Sioux and Cheyenne warriors and was in no mood for compromise when Custer invaded Indian territory.

DON'T BE GREEDY

The Little Bighorn action began on June 25 when the 7th Cavalry, numbering some 700 men, rode upon a massive Native American encampment. It was the largest concentration

BACKGROUND ***"Commanche,"*** *the only U.S. army horse to survive the fighting at Little Bighorn, shown here with his keeper, Trooper Korn, in 1878.*

LEFT ***Crazy Horse, distinguished warrior of the Oglala Sioux*** *and one of the most prominent Native American participants in Little Bighorn. (Painting by Robert Lindneux.)*

of Indians ever assembled on the plains, containing about 10,000 to 15,000 Sioux and Cheyenne, with about 3,000 to 4,000 warriors. Typically, the bold and impatient Custer thought it better to attack immediately without waiting for reinforcements. Colonel John Gibbon had earlier warned him not to be "greedy"—he must have meant "greedy for glory."

Custer divided his regiment into three battalions, sending three companies under Captain Benteen to scout bluffs nearby. Three companies under Major Marcus A. Reno marched on the opposite bank of Little Bighorn River while Custer took five companies toward the north end of the Indian camp. Custer ordered Reno to attack the village from the southern end while he attacked from the north.

However, Custer and Reno woefully underestimated the numbers of warriors they were up against. Scrambling to their horses and grabbing their weapons, a band of Sioux and Cheyenne warriors, including Crazy Horse, threw back Reno's attack, forcing him to retreat across the river to defensive positions on the bluffs beyond, where he was joined by Benteen. In the distance, the Indians could hear heavy gunfire coming from the north end of the valley. With the threat of Reno attacking the village neutralized, the Indians left a few sharpshooters to keep the soldiers on the defensive, while the rest rode back to deal with Custer.

What happened next is largely a mystery as no white man survived the encounter, but it is thought that Custer assumed it would be an easy assault on an unprepared encampment.

DISCOVERING DISASTER

Colonel John Gibbon last saw Custer three days before the battle at Little Bighorn and jokingly warned him not to be greedy while fighting the Sioux and Cheyenne. It was the last time he would see him alive and Gibbon recalls the description of the disaster by an officer reporting back to him:

"He followed Custer's trail to the scene of the battle, opposite the main body of the Indian camp, and amid the rolling hills that border the riverbank on the north. As he approached the ground scattered bodies of men and horses were found, growing more numerous as he advanced. In the midst of the field a long backbone ran out obliquely back from the river, rising very gradually until it terminated in a little knoll which commanded a view of all the surrounding ground, and of the Indian campground beyond the river. On each side of the backbone, and sometimes on top of it, dead men and horses were scattered along. These became more numerous as the terminating knoll was reached, and on the southwestern slope of that lay brave Custer surrounded by the bodies of several of his officers and forty or fifty of his men, whilst horses were scattered about in every direction. All were stripped, and most of the bodies were scalped and mutilated . . . Of Custer there could be no doubt. He was lying in a perfectly natural position as many had seen him lying when asleep, and, we were told, was not at all mutilated, and that, only after a good deal of search the wounds of which he died could be found."

Quoted from ADVENTURES ON THE WESTERN FRONTIER *by John Gibbon, edited by Alan and Maureen Gaff (Indiana University Press, 1994.)*

***Famous and heroic** portrayal of the Battle of Little Bighorn, showing the 7th Cavalry taking up their dismounted defensive position on a hill, with Custer in the center dressed in his frontier clothes, carrying a pistol and holding a wound in his side. (Painting by E. S. Paxson.)*

LEFT *Low Dog, war chief of the Oglala Sioux,* *fought alongside Crazy Horse at Little Bighorn. Although shown in traditional costume, many of the Indians that fought against the 7th Cavalry were armed with repeating rifles that outperformed army issue weapons. (Photo by David F. Barry.)*

However, the Indians were actually gathering an ambush for him and he realized it too late. Superior numbers of Cheyenne and Sioux warriors charged over the river. A running fight followed until the remains of Custer's five companies were surrounded. Some panicked and shot themselves rather than face mutilation at the hands of their enemies. Others dismounted to form a defensive position, but some of their guns jammed and the Indian warriors replied with a hail of arrows and rifle fire before overrunning them and engaging in bitter hand-to-hand fighting. Custer stood on the top of a hill surrounded by some forty to fifty officers and men. None survived.

Reno and Benteen could do little to help Custer and had to defend their position on into the next day until they were relieved by the main column led by Brigadier General Alfred Terry and Colonel Gibbon. Custer's defeat was a savage lesson for an arrogant and overconfident commander. Later, the U.S. army would return with cannons and considerably more men to punish the Indians, but Crazy Horse and his warriors had won a famous victory, even though they wouldn't win the war.

ABOVE *Sioux painting of the Battle at Little Bighorn,* *showing the fight that ensued as the Indian warriors surprised the 7th Cavalry, whose troopers tried to escape before being forced to dismount and take up a defensive position. (Painting by Sioux chief, Red Horse.)*

LITTLE BIGHORN

WAS CUSTER OUTGUNNED at Little Bighorn? This question and other points have been raised by recent archaeological excavation at the battlefield. Exploration of the field in the 1980s revealed a patterning of shell cases that helps reconstruct the battle. Groupings reveal that the final defensive position of Custer's soldiers was a V-shaped formation with Last Stand Hill at its northern point. It also demonstrates that the Indian warriors that Custer fought against were very well armed.

Not only did Custer face numerically overwhelming odds, but it appears he was also caught out by warriors armed with numerous Henry and Winchester repeating rifles. At least sixty-three repeating rifles were used by Indian warriors, making a possible total of some 630 rounds, more than three shots per U.S. soldier. In contrast, the U.S. cavalrymen were armed with trapdoor Springfield single-shot rifles chosen for their performance at long range, but, in close combat, the Springfields were inferior to the repeaters, being notorious for jamming. Few soldiers had time to reload their revolver pistols. Cheyenne warriors claimed that the fighting took only twenty minutes. "It took about as long," said Cheyenne Chief Two Moon, "as it takes a hungry man to eat his dinner."

"Curley" of the Crow tribe, *one of Custer's scouts at Little Bighorn and one of the few to survive the battle.*

To add insult to injury, many of the weapons used by Indian warriors at Little Bighorn had been given to them by the U.S. government. At the Medicine Lodge peace council, Cheyenne tribes-men received trade goods, gunpowder, new revolvers, and several muzzle-loading guns. In his official report on the disastrous battle, Major Reno wondered at the wisdom of this generosity: "The harrowing sight of the dead bodies crowning the height on which Custer fell...is too recent for me not to ask the good people of this country whether a policy that sets opposing parties in the field armed, clothed, and equipped by one and the same government should not be abolished."

PLAN OF BATTLE

Custer fatally divided his force of 700 cavalrymen into three at the beginning of his advance into the Little Bighorn valley in the hope that he could catch the Indian encampment between two attacks: his from the north, and Reno's from the south. Perhaps he hoped it would be like his earlier victory at the Washita, but he had underestimated the number of Sioux and Cheyenne warriors, between 3,000 and 4,000 ready in the encampment. Realizing his mistake too late, he was quickly surrounded.

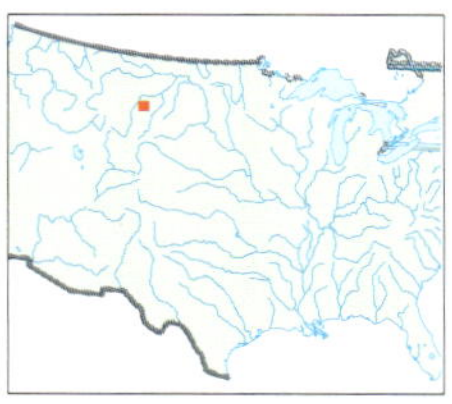

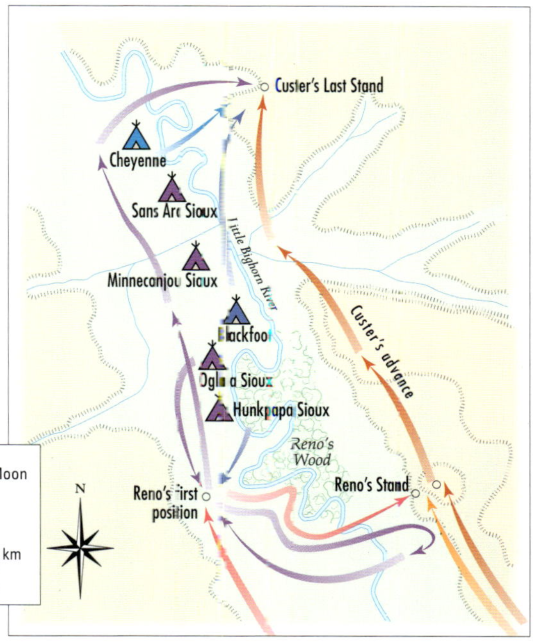

LITTLE BIGHORN

FORMERLY KNOWN AS THE Custer Battlefield National Monument, the park has recently been renamed the Little Bighorn Battlefield National Monument to reflect the Indian view of the battle as well. It lies in the beautiful Wild West landscape of Montana.

Custer Hill

The Last Stand took place here (3), with the cavalrymen shooting their horses to form a barricade behind which they fought to the last man. Custer died here and a headstone bears his name. There is also a monument erected in 1881 that lists the names of all the soldiers killed in the battle.

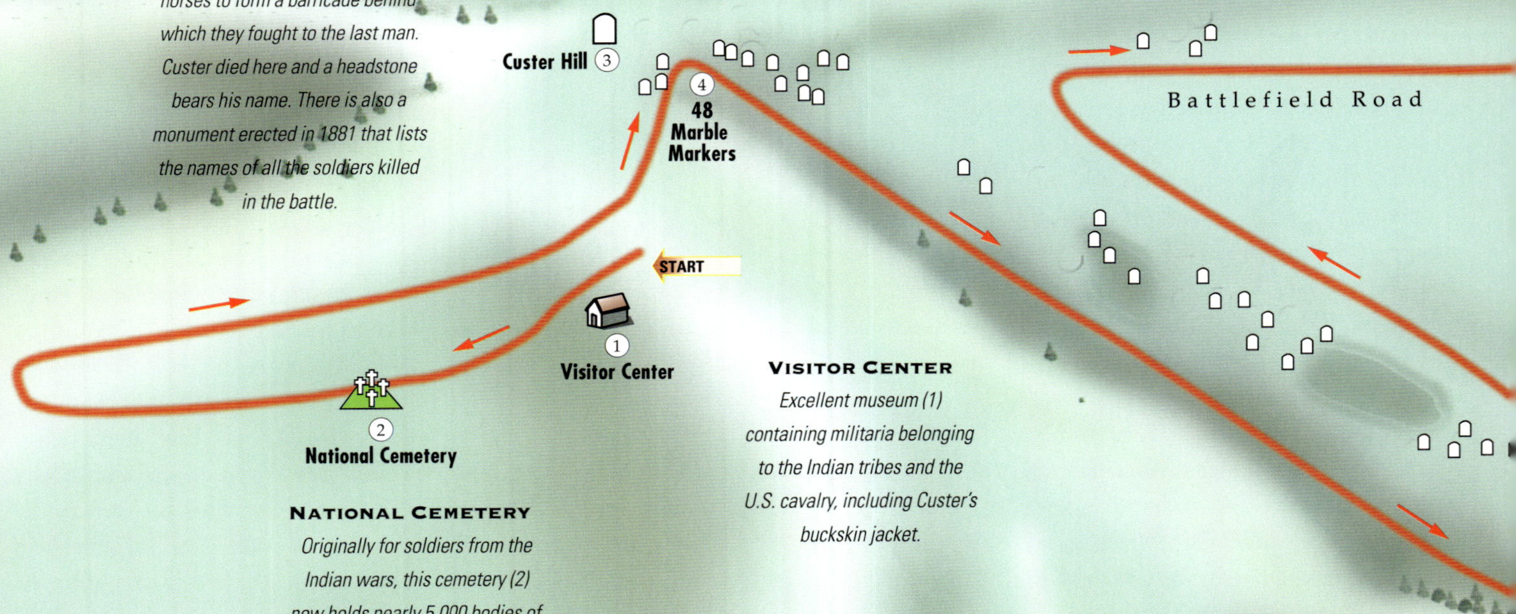

Visitor Center

Excellent museum (1) containing militaria belonging to the Indian tribes and the U.S. cavalry, including Custer's buckskin jacket.

National Cemetery

Originally for soldiers from the Indian wars, this cemetery (2) now holds nearly 5,000 bodies of U.S. soldiers from all major wars of the twentieth century.

BELOW ***Headstones of 7th Cavalry*** *soldiers who died at Little Bighorn clustered together on Custer Hill where the last stand was fought.*

BELOW ***Custer's headstone at Little Bighorn*** *battlefield, showing where his body was found, although his remains were later removed to West Point.*

LEFT *View along Battle Ridge,* *where U.S. cavalrymen were overwhelmed by Crazy Horse's charge.*

BATTLE RIDGE

Marble markers (4) and (6) along Battle Ridge and at Last Stand Hill show the place where bodies were first buried, although they were later all reinterred in a common grave at the monument.

BELOW *Individual marble marker* *noting the ground where this cavalryman fell in the Battle of Little Bighorn.*

DEEP RAVINE

As the 7th U.S. Cavalry fought a running battle away from the pursuing Indians, several soldiers took shelter here (5), and some twenty-eight bodies were later found.

GETTING THERE

LOCATION: *Little Bighorn River, Montana.*

VISITOR INFORMATION: *Little Bighorn Battlefield National Monument, P.O. Box 190, Crow Agency, Montana 59022.*

TELEPHONE: *406 638 2465*

DIRECTIONS: *60 miles east from Billings at intersection of U.S. 90 and 212. Burlington Northern Railroad runs nearby.*

TOUR DISTANCE: *3 miles (5km).*

EUROPE

Europe is the cradle of Western civilization, but this sophistication has been no defense against war which has plagued its land from Istanbul to the Scottish Highlands.

Even those hearts of civilization—the great capitals of Europe—have not been immune, with many of these great cities becoming bitter battlegrounds in the twentieth century, from London to Berlin to Warsaw.

GREATEST CITY ON EARTH

ABOVE *Edirne Gate, through which Mehmet II* *entered the ancient city of Constantinople in triumph.*

LEFT *Mehmet II, conqueror of Constantinople,* *shown as a gentle and refined man. Contemporary portrait attributed to Sinan Bey, c.1475, now in the Topkapi Palace Museum, Istanbul.*

FOR A THOUSAND YEARS CONSTANTINOPLE, the gateway to Asia, had grown rich on trade between Europe and the Middle East. Foreigners were awestruck by its beauty and affluence, many considering it the greatest city on earth. Some of this wealth had been invested in massive fortifications, making it the most impressive bastion of Christendom. Waves of barbarians, including the Huns, had failed to break its formidable defenses.

For much of that time, Constantinople was the capital of the Byzantine Empire, whose rule extended from the Balkans to Syria. Toward the end of this millennium, however, weaknesses appeared in the great capital. The Empire was shrinking and, in 1204, European crusaders stormed its walls, showing that the once mighty city could be taken. By the time the Ottoman Turks arrived in southeastern Europe in the fifteenth century, their leader seriously considered if the time was ripe to make this Christian bulwark the center of his own Muslim empire.

MEHMET THE CONQUEROR

When Mehmet II proposed capturing the city, it was not greeted with enthusiasm by his advisers. The city's immense walls had withstood so many assaults, including previous Turkish attempts and, if he failed, his reputation would be in tatters, leading to attacks on his own position. He was a young man, and had only recently become Sultan.

Constantinople was designed perfectly to withstand a siege. Roughly in the shape of a triangle, its land walls were virtually impregnable; and

BACKGROUND TO BATTLE

The Ottoman Turks came from central Asia and were originally a nomadic people, like the Huns, considered barbaric by their city-based neighbors. As the Byzantine Empire waned, the Turks took over more and more of the Byzantine heartland of Anatolia (now Turkey), gradually controlling more and more land until they stood on the eastern coast of the Aegean Sea and faced Europe.

In the fourteenth century, under the leadership of the Osman family, from whom they gained their dynastic name, the Turks tightened their hold over Anatolia and crossed over into the Balkans, where they fought a number of campaigns culminating in their defeat of the Serbs at Kosovo in 1389. This Muslim victory over the Christian Serbs is still an underlying source of animosity in the Balkans today.

By the beginning of the fifteenth century, the Ottoman Turks dominated southeastern Europe, with their capital at Adrianople (now Edirne), a few miles west of Constantinople. The Byzantine Empire had since shrunk to the city itself, which was now isolated in a Muslim realm. Mehmet II realized the political and geographical weakness of the city and thus took the gamble of laying siege to it.

Background *Mehmet II* *triumphantly enters the ancient city* *of Constantinople. His troops ran wild and pillaged the Byzantine capital.*

the other two sides were surrounded by sea to the south and a natural harbor to the north, so supplies could always find a way into the city. Mehmet was no rash commander—he understood the results of failure and instilled this caution in his own generals. On one occasion he spread a large carpet on the ground and placed an apple in the middle of it. He then asked each of his generals to retrieve it—without setting foot on the carpet. As much as they tried stretching and balancing, they could not get near it. Mehmet then slowly rolled the carpet toward the apple and easily grabbed it. This would be his approach to the siege of Constantinople. Preparation and patience would win him the greatest city in the world.

Mehmet began his preparations by building a castle on the western bank of the Bosphorus, the great waterway to the north of the city that led to the Black Sea. The stone castle, called *Rumeli Hisar*, took just five months to build and gave Mehmet control of one vital route into the city. To make his point he immediately sank a Venetian ship and had its captain impaled, his decaying body left as a warning for the Byzantines within the city. They called upon the rest of the world to help them, but the glory days of Constantinople were long past. The city was now too poor to afford a great mercenary army and no other regional power would risk offending the Turks to help them.

On March 5, 1453, Mehmet invited the city to surrender, and if good sense had prevailed they would have done so, but their commander, Constantine Dragases, the inheritor of the grand title of Emperor, would not give in so easily. His pride and determination encouraged the rest of the capital, and the citizens decided to resist the Ottoman assault. Mehmet assembled an army of 100,000 soldiers, including his 12,000 elite Janissaries, but the most important part of his force was the cannon battery. Artillery had only just come of age in the fifteenth century, playing a vital part

SOLDIERS WITH FLOWERS

The Janissaries were the elite soldiers of the Ottoman Sultan and at Constantinople delivered the final blow to the defenders. Unusually, they were recruited from the sons of conquered families and then trained strictly in the ways of the Ottoman army. Their loyalty and ferocity in battle were legendary and yet Ogier Ghiselin de Busbecq, an Imperial Ambassador to Constantinople, had a different experience of them:

"Janissaries generally visited me in pairs, and, on being admitted to my dining-room, saluted me with a low bow and then hastened, almost ran, towards me and took hold of my garment or hand as though they would kiss it, and offered me a bunch of hyacinths or narcissi. They would then rush back to the door at almost the same speed, taking care not to turn their backs upon me; for this, according to their ideas, is unbecoming. . . Really, if I had not been told that they were Janissaries, I could well have believed that they were a kind of Turkish monk or the members of some kind of sacred association; yet these were the famous Janissaries who carry such terror wherever they go."

From the TURKISH LETTERS OF OGIER GHISELIN DE BUSBECQ, *translated by Edward Seymour Forster (Oxford, 1968).*

Janissaries of the Turkish Ottoman army *on parade. These were the elite warriors of Mehmet's army and took part in the final assault. The symbols on their hats defined their positions and tasks within the army.*

LEFT *Turkish soldiers firing the cannons* *that severely weakened the mighty land walls of Constantinople. (From a painting by J. H. Valda.)*

in the French victory over the English at Castillon, at the end of the Hundred Years War. Mehmet understood the importance of the new military technology and employed a Transylvanian gun-founder who had failed to find service with the Byzantine Emperor. Among the many cannons cast for Mehmet was a monstrous weapon twenty-eight feet long with a bronze barrel eight inches thick that could fire a 12-cwt. ball over a mile. With these cannons in place, Mehmet was ready to take on the great land walls of the city.

TURKISH ASSAULT

The Turkish fleet patrolled the sea to the south of Constantinople, but the Byzantines had protected their harbor to the north of the city, known as the Golden Horn, by securing a massive chain across its entrance. Mehmet began his assault with the roar of his cannon, which opened fire on April 6. Day after day Mehmet's forces pounded the ancient walls, gouging great chunks out of them, but at night the defenders rapidly repaired the damage. A night attack led by Janissaries was stoutly

LEFT *Cannon-damaged area of the land walls* *south of the Topkapi Gate remain unrestored.*

repulsed by the Christian defenders. A convoy of Papal galleys broke through the Turkish fleet and Mehmet's advisers once again warned him of the perils of defeat.

Mehmet needed to strike a devastating blow against the city's defenses to restore his authority. He could see that the entire northern stretch of the city was unthreatened because it lay behind the bay of the Golden Horn. Slaves and soldiers now labored day and night to create a road from the Bosphorus to the northern shore of the Golden Horn. When the road was finished, hundreds of oxen heaved seventy Ottoman ships over land from the Bosphorus to set sail inside the bay of the Golden Horn. The great chain at its entrance had been outflanked, and now Constantinople could be attacked from the north.

Word of a possible Hungarian relief force concentrated Mehmet's thoughts and on May 29 he ordered an all-out attack on the city. Three hours before dawn, 50,000 Turkish warriors assaulted the thin line of defenders on the Land Walls. All the church bells of the city rang the alarm. Irregular troops, recruited from all over the Ottoman empire, flung themselves against the crumbling walls. When they had worn down the defenders, Mehmet led his elite Janissaries into the battle. The defenders fell back from the city walls. The Emperor, clad in armor, tried to rally his men and, with sword in hand, charged among the Turkish warriors, never to be seen again.

Mehmet had finally won his city. At the entrance to St. Sophia, the greatest church in Christendom, he sprinkled a handful of dirt over his turban as a sign of humility. When he entered the church, a soldier was hacking at the marble floor with a sword. "The gold is thine," he said to the warrior, "but the building is mine." The church would have a crescent to replace the cross on its dome and become a mosque. Mehmet who, at just twenty-one years of age, now had his new capital for the Ottoman empire, decided to change the name of Constantinople to the present Istanbul.

ABOVE *Section of the land walls today* *between the Golden and Belgrade Gates, showing the moat and one of the polygonal towers.*

BELOW *Turkish shirt of mail reinforced with plate armor,* *typical of the armor worn by the soldiers attacking Constantinople.*

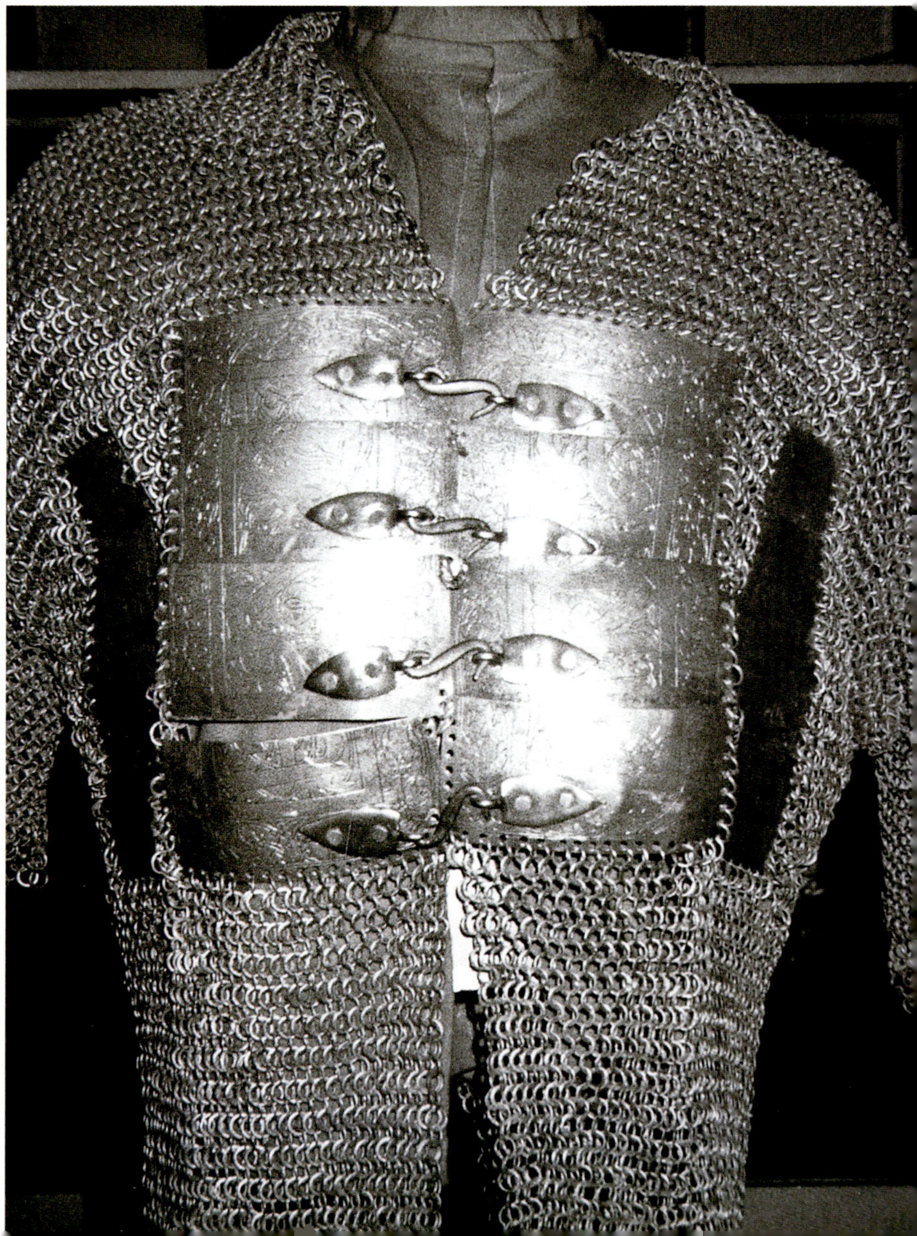

WALLS OF CONSTANTINOPLE

THE WALLS OF Constantinople are extremely well preserved and have recently been the subject of restoration by the Turkish government. It is now possible to walk from one end of the great land walls on the edge of the Golden Horn to the other on the edge of the Sea of Marmara—a distance of about four miles (six and a half kilometers).

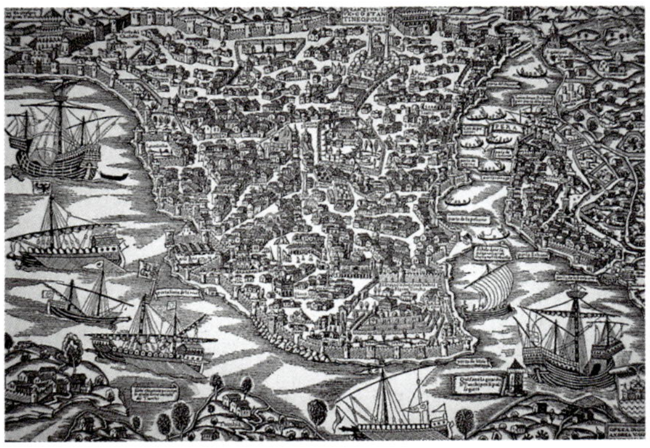

***Contemporary woodcut of Constantinople** showing the land walls at the top, the Imperial Palace at the bottom, and the Golden Horn at the right. Galleys are shown in the Sea of Marmara to the left.*

By the time Mehmet faced the great land walls, they were already a thousand years old, having been built at the time of Emperor Theodosius in 413. An earthquake later demolished much of them, but they were rebuilt with extra fortifications, just in time to dissuade Attila the Hun from attacking the city.

The land walls confronting the Turks consisted of a stone-lined moat sixty feet across, flooded to a depth of thirty feet. Behind this came a walled terrace thirty feet deep—a killing zone for the defenders behind it. The outer wall was nearly thirty feet tall and had ninety-six towers along its length. The main defense, the inner wall, was sixteen feet thick at the base and rose to forty feet above the city. Siege engines were placed on the tops of the towers, able to hurl stones and giant spears at the attackers. Single walls protected the other sides of the city but few remnants of these now remain.

Mehmet directed most of his artillery bombardment against the central portion of the walls near the Topkapi Gate (meaning Gate of the Cannon). His huge guns pounded away until one of the towers flanking the gate was reduced to rubble. Only the quick repairs of the Byzantines prevented this from being a breach through which the Turks could rush.

The middle section of the wall, the Mesoteichion, also suffered badly from Turkish artillery. This section was finally breached on May 29 when the Turks flooded into the city.

PLAN OF BATTLE

The Turks seized control of the Bosphorus when they built the castle of Rumeli Hisar. Their fleet controlled the Sea of Marmara to the south of the city. They had to transport ships across land to capture the Golden Horn, which was enclosed by a great chain or boom. The majority of their 100,000-strong army and artillery were based opposite the great land wall protecting the west side of the city. Approximate figures for the defenders suggest there were barely 5,000 Byzantines and less than 2,000 foreign troops to defend the city.

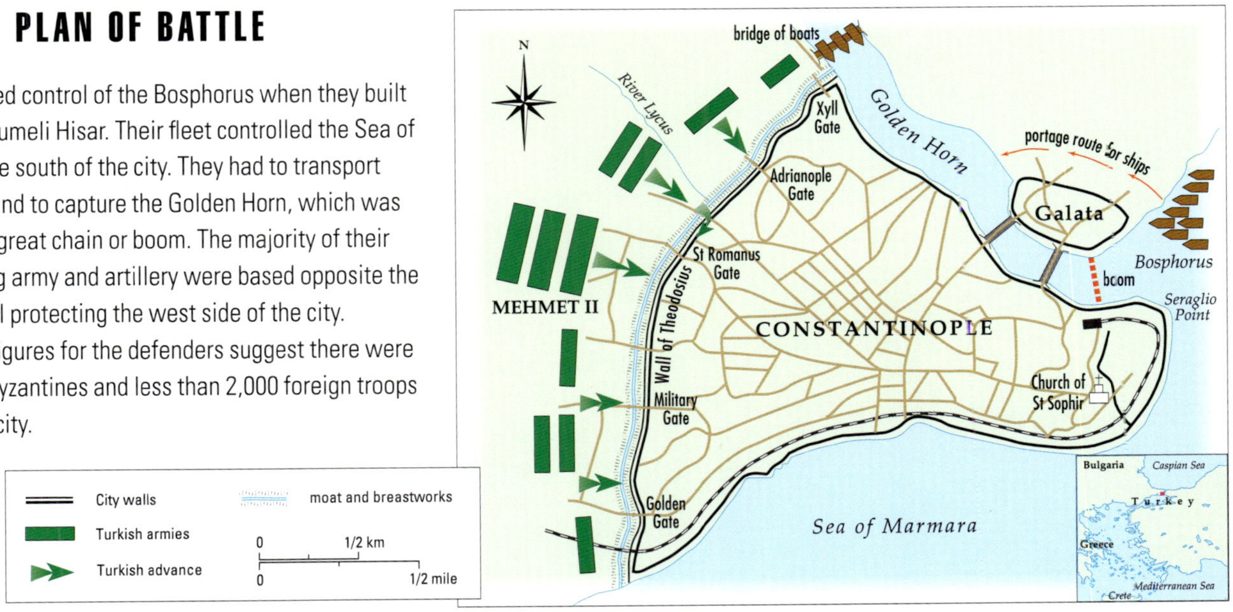

CONSTANTINOPLE

THE CITY OF CONSTANTINOPLE is now known as Istanbul (the name means "Islam Abounds"), which is name the Turks gave to it after conquering it in 1453. It is an ancient city in which three main cultures combine, namely Roman, Byzantine, and Ottoman. By staying in the old city, south of the Golden Horn, one can walk to all the main Muslim, Roman, and Byzantine sites.

ABOVE *One of the finest restored sections* *of the Land Wall near the Belgrade Gate, showing how the inner wall overlooked the outer wall.*

GETTING THERE

LOCATION: *Istanbul, Turkey.*

VISITOR INFORMATION: *Tourism Office, Mesrutiyet Cad. No. 57/1, Galatasayar, Istanbul.*

TELEPHONE: *212 245 01 09*

DIRECTIONS: *The great land walls are to the west of the old city. Reach them by taxi or tour bus from the center of the city.*

TOUR DISTANCE: *The land walls are approximately 4 miles (6.5km) long.*

BELOW *Twin towers* *flanking the Belgrade Gate.*

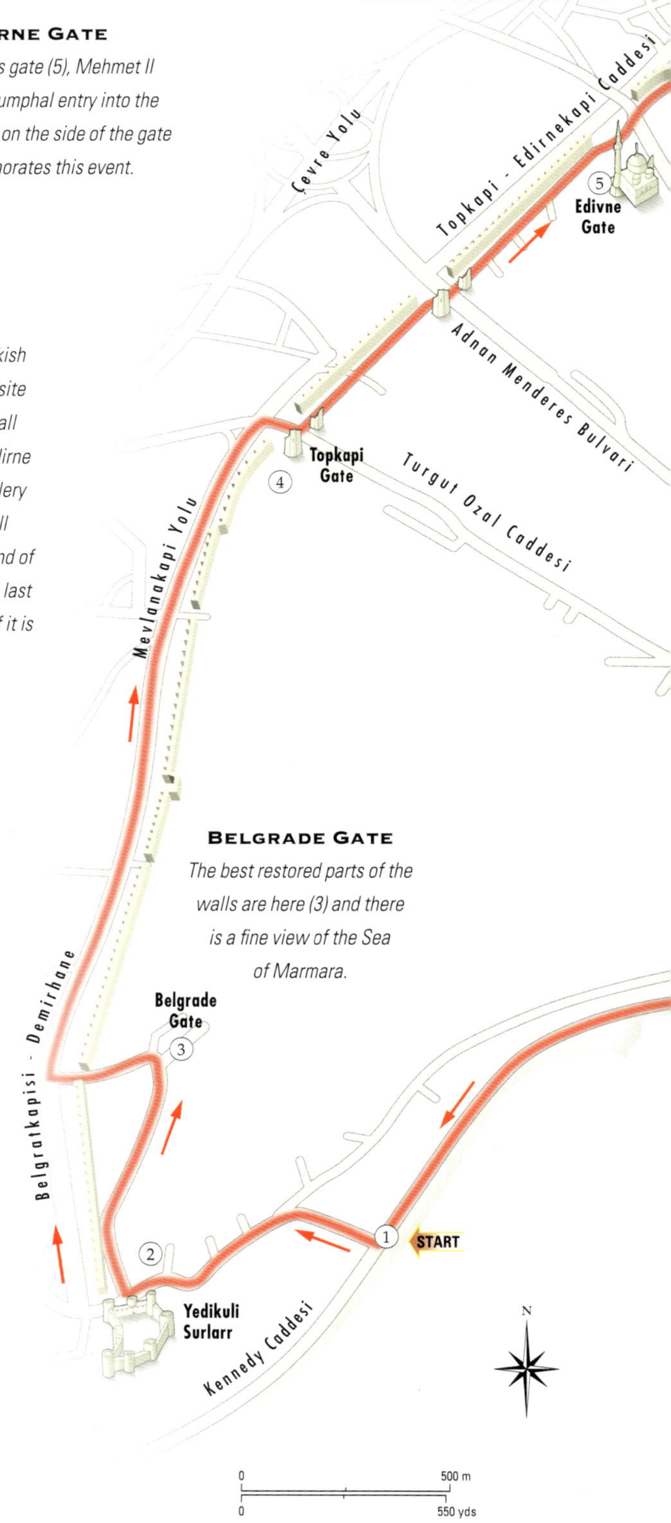

EDIRNE GATE

Through this gate (5), Mehmet II made his triumphal entry into the city. A plaque on the side of the gate commemorates this event.

TOPKAPI GATE

The most powerful of the Turkish cannons were mounted opposite this (4). The stretch of the wall northward from here to the Edirne Gate suffered most from artillery and was the part of the wall breached by the Turks at the end of the siege. It was here that the last Roman Emperor died. Much of it is still damaged today.

BELGRADE GATE

The best restored parts of the walls are here (3) and there is a fine view of the Sea of Marmara.

YEDIKULI

At the southern end of the great land walls, this castle (2) consists of Byzantine towers and Turkish towers built by Mehmet II. The Golden Gate was here, originally a Roman triumphal arch through which emperors paraded. Its gates were once covered in gold, but it was walled up by the time of the Turkish siege.

XYLOKERKOS GATE

This gate (6) was accidentally left open and Turks entered by it. Nearby is the Palace of Porphyrogenitus, one of the last imperial residences in Constantinople.

GOLDEN HORN

The natural harbor of Constantinople (7), its entrance blocked by a great chain during the siege.

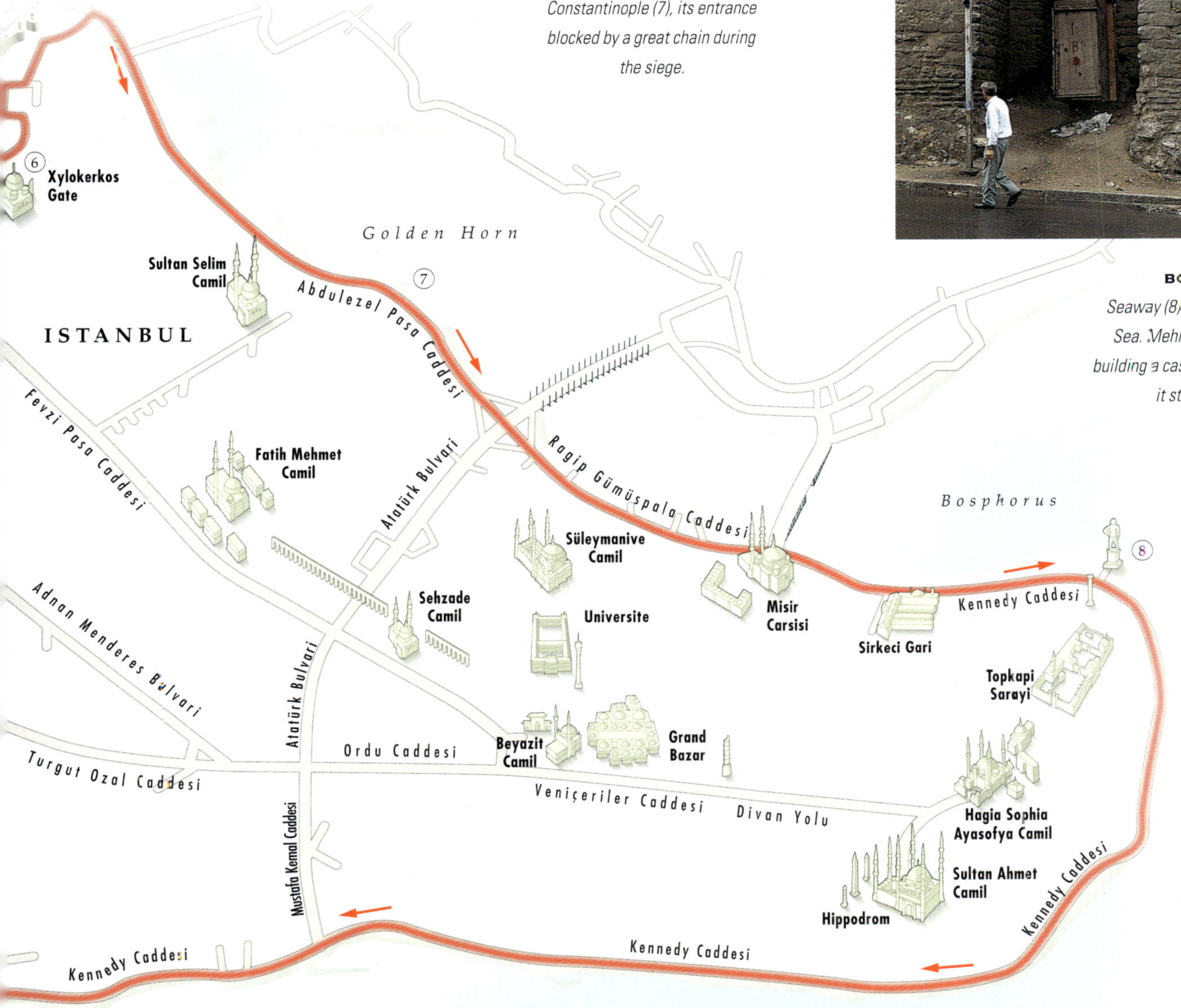

RIGHT ***Porta Xylokerkos,*** *through which a surprise attack was made.*

BOSPHORUS

Seaway (8) that leads to the Black Sea. Mehmet dominated this by building a castle on its western shore; it still stands today.

SEA OF MARMARA

To the south of the city, it was here (1) that a Papal fleet succeeded in breaking through the Turkish ring of ships to bring supplies into the Golden Horn.

RIGHT ***Section of the land walls*** *immediately south of the Belgrade Gate, showing the newly restored towers.*

THE YOUNG PRETENDER

ABOVE ***Memorial cairn*** *at the heart of Culloden battlefield.*

LEFT ***Prince Charles Edward Stuart,*** *also known as Bonnie Prince Charlie, was the Catholic pretender to the English throne and led the Jacobites at Culloden. (From a painting by Le Tocque.)*

PRINCE CHARLES EDWARD STUART, also known as Bonnie Prince Charlie, was the Catholic pretender to the English throne. He claimed descent from the Stuart dynasty that had ruled England in the previous century and was the focal point for anti-Protestant support among European Catholic nations. Supporters of the Stuart cause were called Jacobites (Jacobus being Latin for James, after James II, the last Catholic king of England).

Landing in July 1745 on the shores of a loch near Arisaig in the Scottish Highlands, the Young Pretender gained support from the Scots Highland clans and began his march southward. Initially successful, his victories generated greater support and created fear in England. They marched on through Manchester and Derbyshire. Could this army of rough-and-ready Highlanders really capture London?

King George II despatched his son, William Augustus, Duke of Cumberland, with an army to reassert control of the situation. Faced by overwhelming numbers, Bonnie Prince Charlie retreated to Scotland.

BACKGROUND TO BATTLE

The Jacobite rising of 1745 was planned by the French as a diversion to their own plan to invade England. In 1743 King George II had commanded an army that defeated the French at Dettingen on the continent. Louis XV wanted revenge and raised an army of 12,000 to invade England and set up a Catholic king. He intended to send a smaller force of 3,000 to Scotland with Bonnie Prince Charlie to create a diversionary attack.

In 1744 the French invasion fleet was wrecked by a storm and the invasion was canceled. Bonnie Prince Charlie decided to go it alone to Scotland with a shipment of weapons and £4,000 in gold. In July 1745 he landed near Arisaig but his welcome was muted. Few Highlanders wanted to risk joining him but, at the battle of Prestonpans on September 21, 1745, the Jacobites gained an easy victory over a British army, and success for their cause seemed more possible.

In reality the majority of Scots did not support the Jacobite rebellion, and, increasingly, the subsequent fighting in Scotland assumed the character of a civil war in which Scots fought against Scots rather than the way it has been presented in recent times as a Scottish war of liberation against the English.

As the British advanced north, they sang a song with music written by Henry Purcell and words that declared they would crush "the rebellious Scots" and "God save our gracious King." It was the first appearance of the British national anthem, although the references to the Scots were later tactfully removed.

BATTLE ON THE MOOR

At last, Bonnie Prince Charlie received some good news. The long-promised French troops had landed in Scotland, but disappointingly they were only a few hundred strong. Nevertheless, they, with more Highlanders, inflicted a small defeat on loyalist Highlanders and the rebels felt confident enough to confront King George's army. After the Jacobites scored a final, indecisive victory at Falkirk on January 17, the two forces closed in on each other in April 1746. The Duke of Cumberland commanded an army 9,000 strong, whereas Bonnie Prince Charlie's troops had dwindled to some 5,000.

A key Jacobite supporter, Lord George Murray advised Bonnie Prince Charlie that a night attack might be the best way to get over his side's lack of numbers. But a night attack demands tremendous discipline and the Jacobite army was largely a group of irregular troops, brave in battle, but not trained to execute complex maneuvers. The British army was based at Nairn, along the coast from Inverness in the far northeast of Scotland. The Scots chose to attack on the eve of the Duke of Cumberland's birthday as they anticipated that the British would be merry and drunk from celebrating with their commander. The night was pitch black and the ground leading to Nairn was rough. The Scots' formations began to break up in the darkness and, hopelessly muddled, they decided to call off the assault half way through the night. Exhausted and demoralized, the Scots returned to their camp on Culloden Moor, many of them instantly falling to sleep on the ground.

Contrary to the Scots' expectations, the

BELOW *Contemporary print of the battle of Culloden,* *showing the Duke of Cumberland in the foreground.*

British soldiers toasted their commander with brandy, but they then went straight to sleep and rose early at 4:00 A.M., ready to march on Inverness. Hearing that the Scots were asleep on top of Culloden Moor, the British prepared themselves for battle. Dragging themselves from their sleep, the Scots could do little but watch as the British deployed themselves into their battle formations. Battle began finally at 1.00 P.M.

REDCOATS AND JACOBITES

The British Army consisted of fifteen infantry battalions arranged in three lines, with three regiments of cavalry mainly on the left flank, a total of nearly 6,000 soldiers. Field guns were placed in the gaps between the battalions with the second-line battalions covering the gaps between the battalions in the first line. Bonnie Prince Charlie's Jacobite army comprised mainly of Scots Highlanders organized in three lines, among them the clans of the Camerons, Frasers, MacLeans, MacLachlans, and MacDonalds, some 3,800 warriors. Two small regular units of French troops stood in reserve with a handful of cavalry.

The battle began with the rebels firing their cannons. The British replied and the Highlanders, with typical impatience, surged forward. This charging attack was known as the Highland Charge and was not as reckless as it might have seemed. It had worked previously in confrontations with the British in which the clansmen had reduced their exposure to cannon fire by running quickly across the battlefield, and this aggression, combined with war cries, had unnerved the British sufficiently so that they broke formations and then became vulnerable to hand-to-hand fighting. On this occasion, however, the British were not so easily intimidated. They did not run, and the Highlanders found themselves met by disciplined volleys of fire.

The British artillery changed its ammunition from cannonballs to canister shot, which exploded like the charge from giant

BELOW *British soldiers hunt Jacobite rebels after Culloden.* *Much has been made of the brutality of the British, but both sides were equally ruthless, showing no quarter to the enemy. (From a painting by Seymour Lucas.)*

shotguns on the running Scotsmen. Several of the clans' leading men fell dead, and the Highland Charge faltered. Moments later, the Jacobites were hit by volleys of musket fire. A British soldier described what happened next: "When we saw them coming towards us in great haste and fury, we fired at about fifty yards distance, which made hundreds fall; notwithstanding which, they were so numerous, that they still advanced, and were almost upon us before we had loaded again. We immediately gave them another full fire."

The two sides then clashed, with Highlanders using swords and shields against British soldiers armed with bayonets on the end of their muskets. The Jacobites broke through the first line of battalions, but were met by the fire and bayonets of the second line. All along the British line, the Duke of Cumberland's troops kept their order and poured volleys into the Scots. Stunned by the fusillade, the Jacobite left wing stopped on the boggy ground and refused to close with the redcoats. The Jacobite right wing broke and fled, chased by the British cavalry. The French reserve fired one volley, then decided it was better to retreat.

Bonnie Prince Charlie was devastated and tried to rally his men, but his advisers told him to quickly leave the battlefield. His dreams of a Catholic kingdom in Britain were over, and so was the last great military campaign on British soil. Of the rebels, 1,500 were dead or wounded, with the British suffering only 300 casualties. There was little mercy for the defeated Scots because they had ruthlessly slaughtered beaten British soldiers in the past and, before this battle, Cumberland had ordered no quarter. The British were little inclined to take prisoners. Bonnie Prince Charlie set sail for France where he stayed, and the British kingdom was never again troubled by Jacobite pretenders.

BACKGROUND *Handle of broadsword used by Donald Cameron of Lochiel* *at the battle of Culloden. Cameron was wounded but escaped to France.*

DEADLY FIRE

At Culloden, the Jacobite Highlanders hoped to repeat their earlier successes in which the British had lost their nerve in the face of the Highland Charge. As Michael Hughes, a British eyewitness, recalled, they seemed genuinely surprised by the ferocity of redcoat resistance and fire:

"Making a dreadful huzza, and even crying 'Run, ye dogs!', they [the Highlanders] broke in between the [British] grenadiers of Barrel and Monro; but these had given their fire according to the general direction, and then parried them with their screwed bayonets. The two cannons on that division were so well served, that within two yards of them they [the rebels] received a full discharge of cartridge shot, which made a dreadful havoc; and those who crowded into the opening received a full fire from the centre of Bligh's regiment, which still increased the number of the slain. However, such as survived possessed themselves of the cannon and attacked the regiments sword in hand."

Quoted in 1745: A MILITARY HISTORY OF THE LAST JACOBITE RISING *by Stuart Reid (Spellmount, 1996).*

British soldiers, including grenadiers, *armed with muskets tipped with bayonets, clash with Highlanders during the Jacobite revolt of 1745. Bayonets helped the British cope with the fearsome Highland Charge in which the Scots liked to close quickly for hand-to-hand fighting. (From a painting by Morier.)*

CULLODEN MOOR

Culloden Moor lies on top of a broad ridge running from east to west, approximately five miles east of Inverness. On one side of the moor lay two stone-walled enclosures, and on the other were the walls of the Culloden Parks, part of the estate from which the battle derived its name. It is an inhospitable windswept land and the ground is waterlogged. One rebel, James Johnstone, remembered it being so boggy that it affected his movements: "Having charged on foot and in boots I was so overcome by the marshy ground, the water on which reached to the middle of the leg, that instead of running I could scarcely walk."

The boggy land must have had a tremendous impact on the traditional running attack of the Jacobite Highlanders, making it much more exhausting for them to cross the moor and close with the enemy, thus reducing their energy and enthusiasm for hand-to-hand fighting. The wet land also influenced the disposition of the British, for Cumberland placed his cavalry on drier ground on his left flank simply because it was much firmer. British artillery appear to have been ordered to fire their cannon balls higher because if they fell short they would just stick in the ground rather than bouncing to cause damage. Many rebels remembered the initial cannonballs flying harmlessly over their heads. Most of the artillery damage was caused at very close range.

Despite these problems, the Scots still started the battle with a stirring charge, as one eyewitness recalled: "They broke from the center in three large bodies like wedges, and moved forward...and after firing very irregularly at a considerable distance, they rushed furiously in upon them [the British], thinking to carry all before them, as they had done on former occasions."

Visiting the battlefield today evokes clearly the difficult conditions under which both sides fought. In 1746, the field was covered with grass rather than heather, as it was used for rough grazing by the local estate. Some of the original walls that defined the battlefield have been reconstructed. Many soldiers were buried together on the field of battle, and so the moor today retains the aura of sacred land.

One must, however, beware of the Scottish myths that have since grown up around the battlefield. Old Leanach cottage was traditionally believed to be the place where wounded Jacobite soldiers were burned alive in a barn. In fact, the cottage itself has been dated back to only 1760, and the original farm is thought to have been used as a British Army field hospital.

PLAN OF BATTLE

The Jacobites formed into three lines, with the majority of troops in the first line, some 3,800 strong. Small French units and a handful of cavalry stood in reserve. The British Army of fifteen battalions formed in two lines, with the second line overlapping the gaps in the first. Substantial cavalry stood on its left wing. When the battle began, the Highland Charge worked most successfully against Barrell's unit, overrunning it, but any breakthrough was sealed off by units in the British second line. Under pressure of fire, the clans panicked and broke.

Jacobite Army position
Turf dyke line
Tracks
Viewpoints
Government Army position
0 300 m
0 400 yds

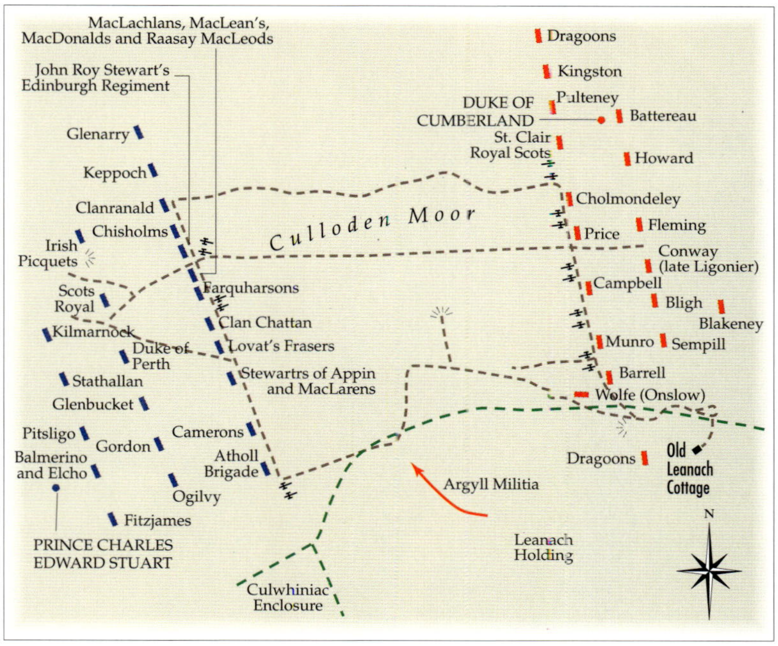

CULLODEN MOOR

WINDSWEPT, WATERLOGGED, AND BROODING, Culloden Moor is a fitting memorial to the disastrous end of the Jacobite cause. The bodies of many Highland warriors lie buried beneath the long grass, and so the ground today is undisturbed by development.

GETTING THERE

LOCATION: *Culloden Moor, near Inverness, Scotland.*

VISITOR INFORMATION: *Visitor Centre, National Trust for Scotland, Culloden Moor, Inverness IV2 5EU.*

TELEPHONE: *01463 790 607*

DIRECTIONS: *By car, five miles (8km) east of Inverness, following the B9006.*

TOUR DISTANCE: *1½ miles (2.5km).*

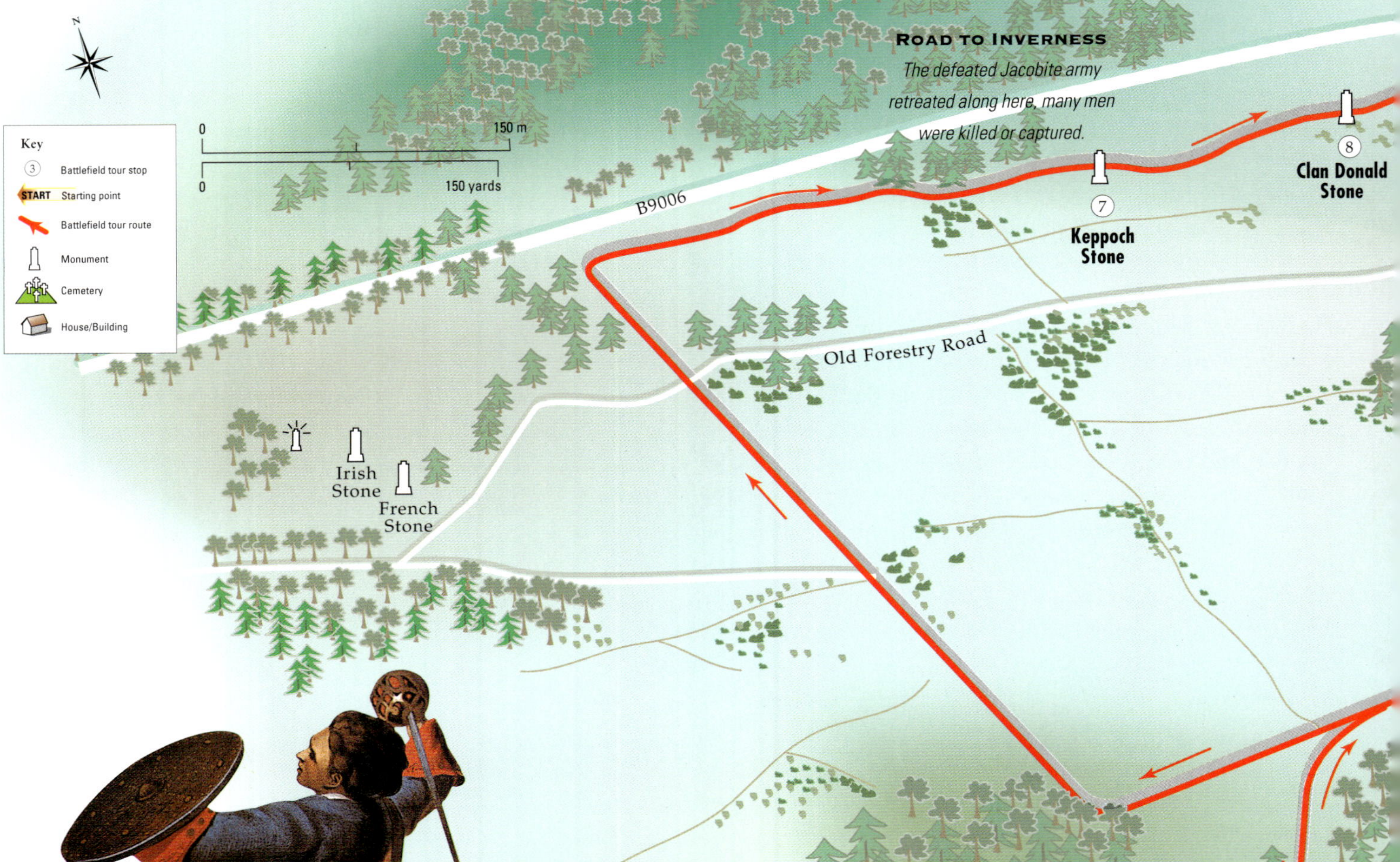

ROAD TO INVERNESS

The defeated Jacobite army retreated along here, many men were killed or captured.

CULWHINIAC

The British cavalry broke through the stone walls of these enclosures (6) to attack the Jacobite army on its right flank.

LEFT *Major Gillies MacBean,* *a Highland officer killed at Culloden. (Painting by McIan.)*

Graves of the Clans (4)
Memorial stones commemorating the clans of the Stewarts (left) and the MacGillivrays (right).

Below *Old Leanach Cottage (3)*
The British positions ran northwest from this cottage. It was near here that the Highlanders overran Barrell's unit and broke through the first line, but were stopped by the second British line. It was the turning point of the battle. The cottage is thought to have been used as a British Army field hospital. A Visitor Center (2) is nearby, providing an exhibition, a short film, and a restaurant.

Right *Highland warrior with broadsword* *and round shield or targe, typical of those who fought at Culloden, although many were also armed with pistols and muskets. (Painting by Mclan.)*

THEY SHALL NOT PASS

ABOVE *French soldiers* *shown wearing body armor and carrying weapons, including grenades, needed for close-combat fighting in the bitter trench warfare of the Western Front.*

LEFT *Ossuare de Douaumont and cemetery*, *the Ossuary was opened in 1932. Some of the 15,000 graves in the cemetery can be seen before it.*

THE FORTRESS CITY OF VERDUN was not of vital importance on the Western Front. If it had been abandoned, it would have straightened and shortened the French line. Indeed, many of the guns had been removed from its bastions to be positioned elsewhere. But for ten months in 1916, Verdun became hell on earth as the French army bled itself white in its determination not to give up before the Germans.

The concept behind the German assault on Verdun seemed to be not so much a key to invading France, but more a symbolic act for challenging French morale. It was to become the anvil on which the Germans would strike their hammer of attrition. Erich von Falkenhayn's offensive was intended to cause so many casualties to the French that they would suffer a loss of will to carry on fighting.

BACKGROUND TO BATTLE

General Erich von Falkenhayn became chief of the German General Staff in September 1914. He took over from Helmuth von Moltke who had been behind the initial war of maneuver, based on the Schlieffen plan, which had enabled the Germans to sweep through Belgium, only to be stopped by the Allies at the River Marne. Moltke's failure and the stagnation of the Western Front left Falkenhayn with no illusions about the enormity of his task.

Falkenhayn surveyed the enemies he faced and made sharp judgments on them all. The Russians had lost their ability to attack. The British were the main power to fear, and they seemed almost impossible to defeat. Their mastery of sea power meant they could not be invaded; and on the Western Front in Flanders, they were defended by trenches and mud. The only way to fatally wound Britain was to knock out its principal ally—France.

Falkenhayn believed that the French will to fight had been tested to the point of breaking, and that one mighty assault would finally shatter it. The choice of Verdun for this attack was perhaps also influenced by the Franco-Prussian War, forty years earlier, as it had been lost to the Germans in 1870 and not returned until three years later.

GERMAN OFFENSIVE

After several postponements, the first German blow fell on February 21, 1916. A nine-hour artillery bombardment was unleashed, building in intensity. At around 4:00 P.M. the barrage ceased, and German infantry of Crown Prince Wilhelm's Fifth Army emerged from their trenches and rushed across no-man's-land. Despite being shocked by the ferocity of the artillery, the French of the Third Army stood in their positions to give stiff resistance to the Germans. By nightfall both sides had endured heavy casualties. The next day, the Germans pressed on, making short gains and following up with heavy bombardment of the French lines. After four days these costly tactics bore some fruit as the greatest of Verdun forts, Douaumont, was overrun.

French General Henri Pétain was given overall command of the French forces at Verdun and he reinforced them with his Second Army plus extra artillery and aircraft brought from elsewhere along the line. It is Pétain who is popularly credited with uttering the phrase "They shall not pass!", demonstrating his commitment to holding Verdun. The German gamble that the French would not give up Verdun had been right, but they too were suffering from this determination and, by the end of February, German advances had halted. French flanking fire from the west bank of the Meuse was proving effective, and supplies poured into Verdun. The Germans now reinforced their positions with extra troops on their right and left flanks, launching heavy attacks on the west bank of the Meuse. By May 6, the German Fifth Army had advanced as far as Avocourt and Chattencourt.

VIVE LA FRANCE!

The French launched bitter counterattacks, which soaked up bodies on both sides, but the Germans pressed on. On June 1 five German divisions attacked Fort Vaux. Its plucky commander, Major Silvain-Eugène Raynal, demonstrated the courage that the French exhibited throughout the long battle. He estimated that between 1,500 and 2,000

MAKING THE EARTH QUAKE

German artillery assaults at Verdun were intended to break the spirit as much as the bodies of the men they bombarded. A French machine-gun sergeant of the Twenty-sixth Infantry Regiment recalls how terrible they were:

> "The pounding was continuous and terrifying. We had never experienced its like during the whole campaign. The earth around us quaked, and we were lifted and tossed about. Shells of all calibers kept raining on our sector. The trench no longer existed, it had been filled with earth. We were crouching in shell-holes, where the mud thrown up by each new explosion covered us more and more. The air was unbreathable. Our blinded, wounded, crawling and shouting soldiers kept falling on top of us and died while splashing us with their blood. It really was a living hell. How could one ever survive such moments? We were defeated, dizzy, and sick at heart. It is hard to imagine the torture we endured: our parched throats burned, we were thirsty, and the bombardment seemed endless."

Quoted in VERDUN *1916 by Malcolm Brown (Tempus, 1999).*

German incendiary bombs *drop on the ancient city of Verdun, causing devastating fires. (Painting by François Flameng.)*

BACKGROUND *Typical French infantry* *of the type that fought at Verdun. They wear the "casque Adrian," a steel antishrapnel helmet, and "horizon blue" greatcoats.*

artillery shells hit his fort every hour. Holding barricade after barricade inside the corridors of the fort, Raynal slowly retreated, at times he and his men fighting on in gas masks as poison gas and flame-throwers were used upon them. Finally, it was a lack of water that forced Raynal and his men to surrender after a week, their last message being "Vive la France!" As they accepted his capitulation, the Germans informed Raynal that he had been awarded the Légion d'Honneur by his government.

On June 24, following the British attack at the Somme, the Germans ceased supplying reinforcements and ammunition to Verdun. The threat to capture Verdun was now over, and the Germans relied on defensive tactics. The French launched more counterattacks and slowly but surely recaptured the ground lost in the spring. Advancing behind creeping barrages (heavy artillery fire concentrated on the enemy line, enabling the infantry to advance), the French took back all their symbolic losses.

On October 24 Fort Douaumont was retaken, plus ground that had taken the Germans four months to capture. On November 2 Fort Vaux was recaptured, and on

BELOW *German stormtrooper armed with grenades* *to blow up bunkers during quick advances on French trenches. A steel defensive plate used during trench warfare is shown near his foot.*

December 15 a final French offensive returned their front line to almost the same position it has been forced back from in February.

In their strategic aims the Germans had failed. Both sides had suffered terribly. Estimates at losses are around 377,000 French killed, wounded, or missing, and 337,000 German casualties. Nine villages that had stood on the soil of the battle for a thousand years, were completely destroyed and never rebuilt. Parts of the farming land were so poisoned by explosives and dead bodies that they were simply planted with trees and not cultivated again. The morale of both sides was badly dented by the struggle, reinforcing the awful futility of attrition warfare on the Western Front.

BELOW *German casualties of French counterattacks* *during the battle of Verdun.*

RIGHT *Remains of Fort Douaumont*, *major stronghold of the French position at Verdun.*

VERDUN

General Henri Pétain, *commander of French forces at the battle of Verdun, shown in his mobile headquarters on board a train.*

The battlefield of Verdun is dominated by the belts of concrete forts begun in the late nineteenth century, marking the frontier defenses of France following its defeat by Germany in 1870. They are low-lying gun emplacements typical of the period. At first, they were built from stone surrounded by earth ramparts, but the development of high explosives saw a further shell of concrete added to them. Artillery guns were placed inside armored steel turrets on top of them.

Despite this, before 1916, similar forts had proved useless against heavy bombardment, one fort being forced to surrender because the fumes of imploding shells made it impossible to hold. For this reason, many of the more easily movable guns were removed from the forts. At Verdun, the position in front of the city was commanded by the major fortress of Douaumont and the smaller fortress of Vaux. These two fortresses can be visited today and form the center of the commemorations to the battle. Tours are conducted inside the galleries and casemates of the fortresses.

Raynal, the heroic French commander of Vaux, described the conditions inside the fort that finally brought the end to their remarkable defense: "The door suddenly opened. There stood a terrifying apparition. It was a wounded man, his naked chest swathed in bloody bandages. He leaned with one hand against the door frame, and thrusting out a leg, went down on one knee. He held out his other hand in a supplicating gesture, and in a whisper, muttered: 'Mon commandant, something to drink...' It was the end. Unless a miracle happened, this would be the last night of our resistance. My men, who drank no more, ate no more, slept no longer, only held themselves upright by a prodigy of will."

Near Douaumont, the Tranchée des Baïonnettes was a sector of the French front-line trenches into which fifty-seven soldiers disappeared during a bombardment. Three years later they were found again, when a line of rusting bayonets and rifles was noticed to be protruding from an earth-filled trench in this sector. Today this infamous trench is covered by a concrete canopy, and the bodies of those soldiers still unidentified are marked by wooden crosses.

PLAN OF BATTLE

Verdun and its double ring of forts formed a salient on the river Meuse. Crown Prince Wilhelm's Fifth Army attacked all along the front line around Verdun on February 21. The French Third Army was reinforced by the Second Army under the command of Henri Pétain, and counterattacked toward the middle of the German line around the strongly contested forts of Douaumont and Vaux. During ten months of fighting, some 37 million German and French shells were fired. More than 700,000 men became casualties.

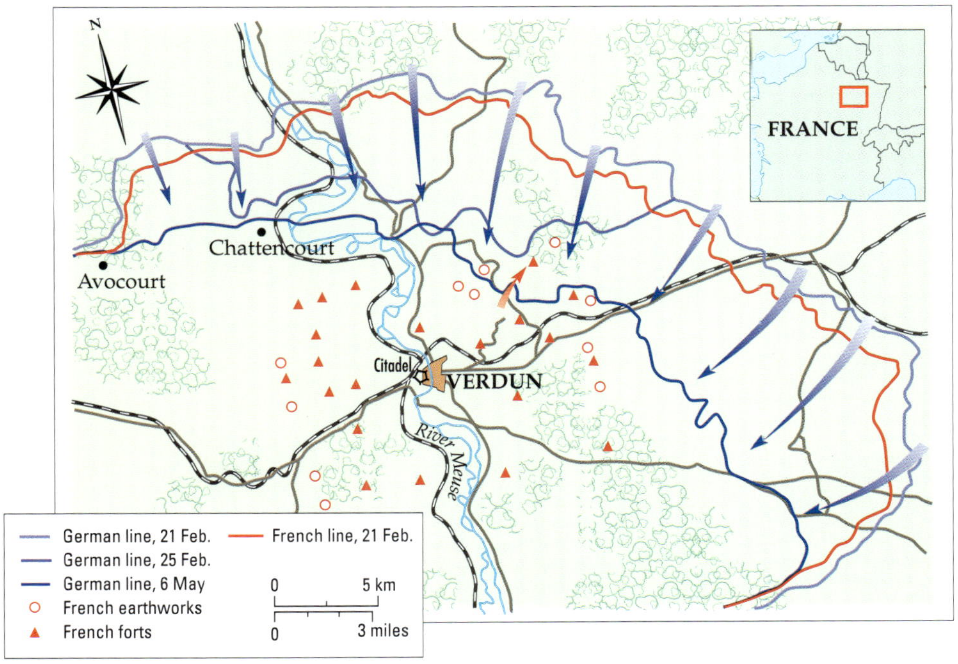

VERDUN

VERDUN IS A BUSY PROVINCIAL CITY that will form the base for your tour of the battlefield. The crumbling steel and concrete forts of Vaux and Douaumont set the character for this grim story of endurance and defiance.

ABOVE *French officers in headquarters* *dug below the earth of the Western Front as protection against artillery bombardments.*

GETTING THERE

LOCATION: *Verdun, northern France.*

VISITOR INFORMATION: *French Tourist Office, Place du Nation, 55 100, Verdun.*

TELEPHONE: *03 2986 1418*

DIRECTIONS: *By car, leave Verdun eastward by N3, then turn left onto D913 toward Fort Vaux.*

TOUR DISTANCE: *16.5 miles (26km).*

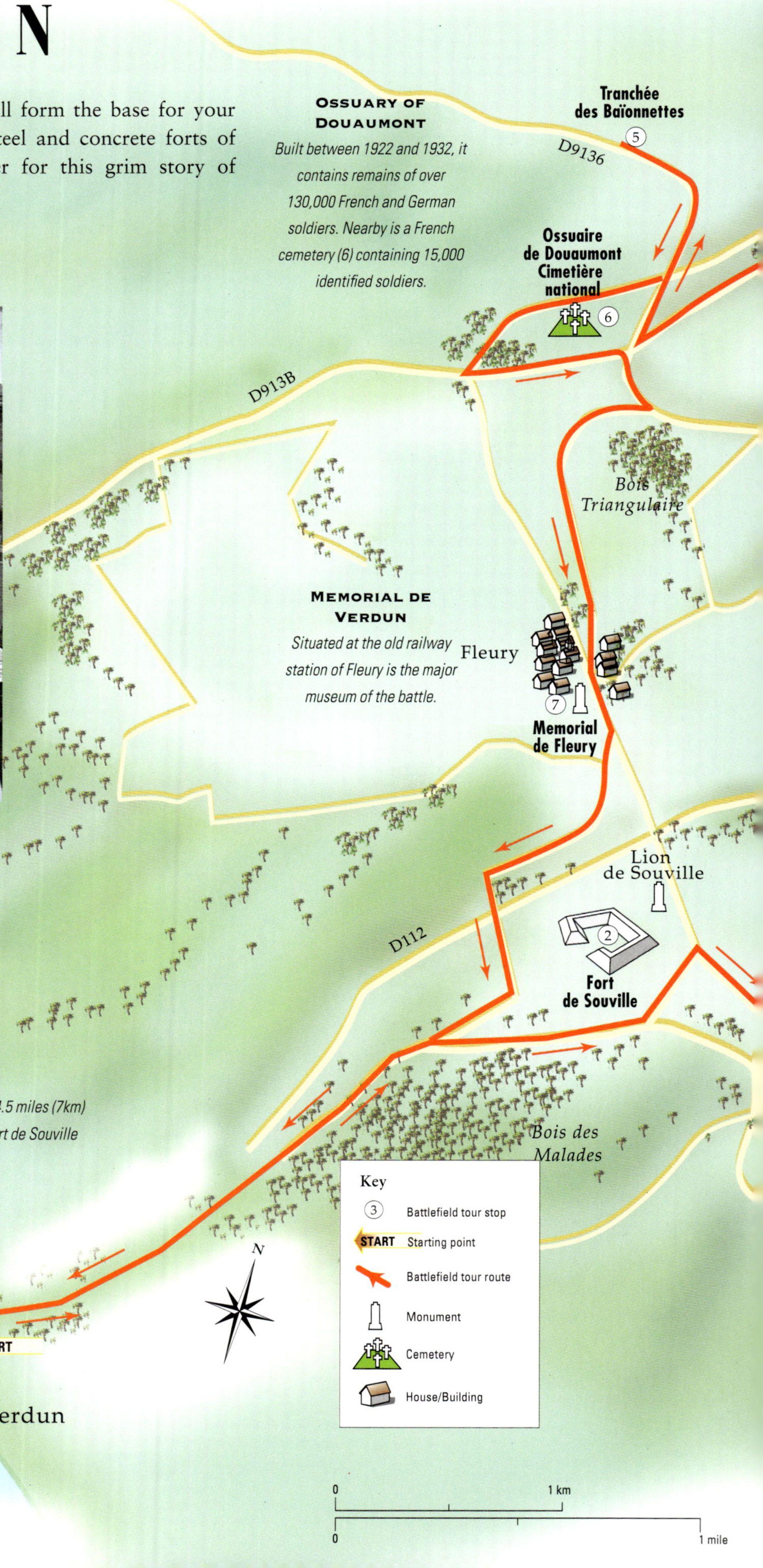

TRANCHÉE DES BAÏONNETTES
The trench (5) in which French soldiers were buried during a bombardment.

OSSUARY OF DOUAUMONT
Built between 1922 and 1932, it contains remains of over 130,000 French and German soldiers. Nearby is a French cemetery (6) containing 15,000 identified soldiers.

MEMORIAL DE VERDUN
Situated at the old railway station of Fleury is the major museum of the battle.

Map not to scale: 4.5 miles (7km) from Verdun to Fort de Souville

Fort Douaumont

The major fort in this area (4) was captured by the Germans and then recaptured by the French.

Above Fort Douaumont, *showing one of the surviving steel machine-gun cupolas.*

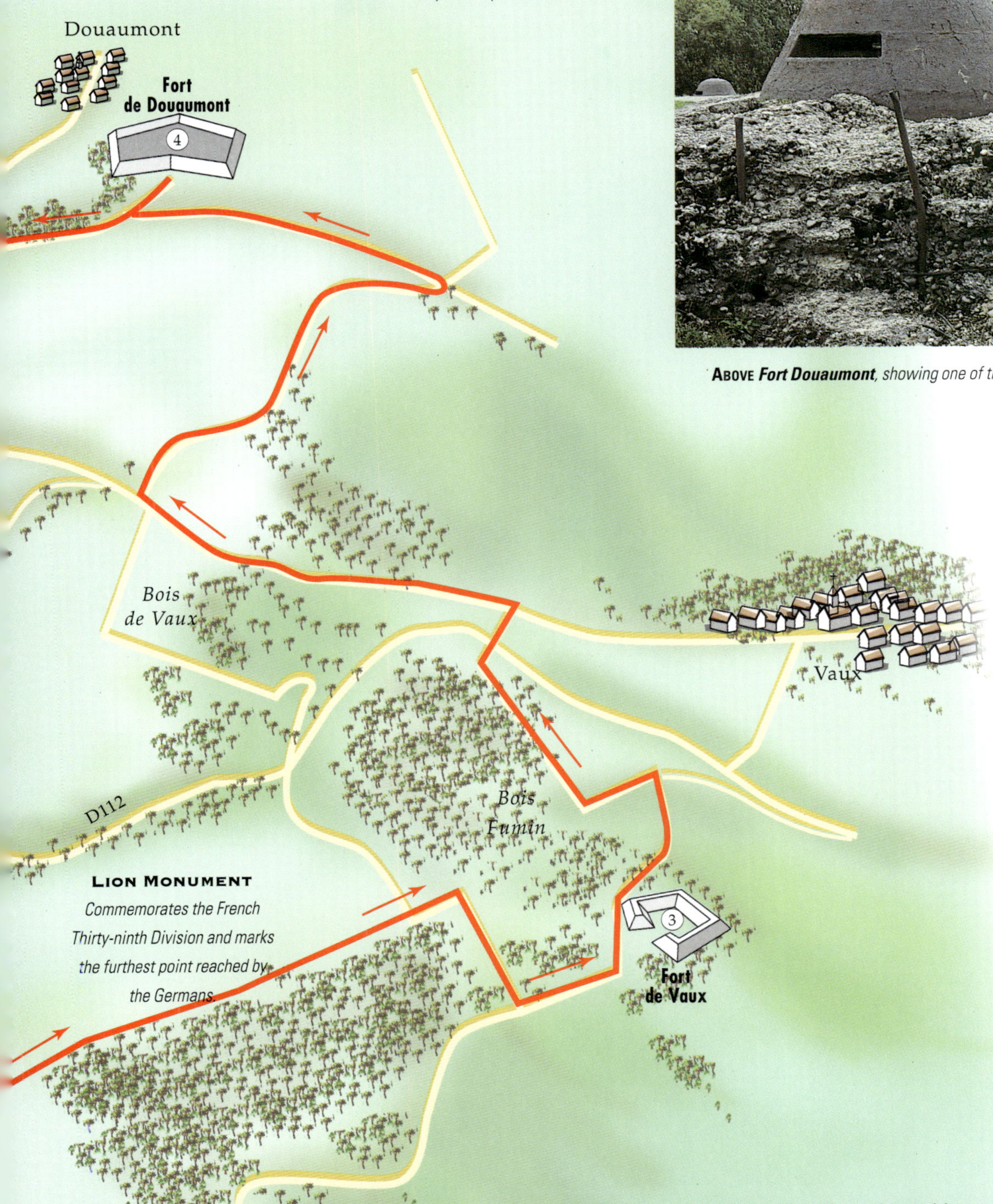

Lion Monument

Commemorates the French Thirty-ninth Division and marks the furthest point reached by the Germans.

Fort de Vaux

Commandant Raynal led an heroic defense of this fort (3) against the Germans. On its walls is a memorial to the pigeon that carried the last message from Raynal before he was captured. Both Raynal and the last pigeon from Fort Vaux were awarded the Légion d'Honneur for valor.

Preserved trenches *near Verdun, one of the more poignant remnants of the battle.*

Fort de Souville, *another surviving stronghold of the French position near Verdun.*

SUCCESS ON THE WESTERN FRONT

Above *Canadian artillery assist in the preliminary* *bombardment that opened the battle of Arras-Vimy in April 1917. (Painting by Kenneth H. Forbes.)*

Left *Canadian Memorial* *at Vimy Ridge above Hill 145.*

Fighting on the Western Front in World War I is so frequently depicted as a tragic tale of brave soldiers bogged down in mud and overwhelmed by modern firepower, but at the battle of Arras, culminating with the capture of Vimy Ridge, the story is one of professional success. Poor generalship and inadequate tactics are often blamed for the high loss of life on the Western Front, but this presumes that little had been learned in the four years of war. On the contrary, the generals and their officers worked hard to devise methods that would reduce the rate of casualties. At Arras and Vimy Ridge this bore fruit spectacularly.

BITTER LESSONS LEARNED

The slaughter of the Somme in the previous year has been caused in part by a misunderstanding of the use of artillery. It had been presumed that a massive artillery barrage before an attack would silence any opposition, but the reality proved that artillery shells failed to destroy barbed wire or deeply buried machine-gun posts. When the British infantry attacked, they became the victims of a tragic misjudgment.

By Arras in April 1917 these bitter lessons had been learned. The numbers, range, and accuracy of British artillery had been greatly improved during the winter. They could now take on the enemy artillery and even isolate front-line troops by bombing their supply lines. The

BACKGROUND TO BATTLE

Although the Germans had savagely dented Allied attempts at a breakthrough on the Western Front at the Somme, they too had suffered terribly both at the Somme and Verdun. German commanders could see there would be no decisive victory on the Western Front and decided to fight a defensive war, withdrawing to the heavily fortified Hindenburg Line.

The Allied offensive at Arras and Vimy Ridge was a response to the German retreat, hoping to break through the German defenses north of the Hindenburg Line and outflank the new positions. The French, having suffered catastrophically at Verdun and shaken by mutinies spreading through their army, were happy for the British to extend their command of the Western Front in France.

British had also devised the creeping barrage, in which the artillery would lay down walls of fire some 2,000 yards ahead of the advancing infantry. On top of this, there was the massed use of machine guns, poison gas projectors, and tanks. At Arras–Vimy on April 9, there were eighteen infantry divisions backed by 2,817 artillery guns, 2,340 gas projectors, and sixty tanks. The preliminary bombardment lasted for three weeks, building up in the last five days before zero hour to an enormous barrage.

Generalship was also good. The British commander was General Edmund Allenby and, although he was denied his use of surprise by supreme commander, General Sir Douglas Haig, such were his battlefield organizational skills that the subsequent triumph must be attributed in part to him. Later failures to exploit this success saw him run afoul of his feud with Haig and he was transferred to the war backwater of Palestine. But there he proved to be a brilliant leader, using blitzkrieg tactics to defeat the Turks in a series of spectacular victories.

ABOVE *A massive 9.2-caliber British howitzer.* *The creeping barrage, in which artillery shells were dropped just before advancing Allied infantry, was a decisive tactic during the fighting at Arras and Vimy Ridge.*

NOT MUCH ROMANCE

At the beginning of the battle some of the British were helped by a warren of ancient tunnels at Arras that enabled them to advance to the battlefield under cover. Lieutenant D. W. J. Cuddeford, commanding a company of the Twelfth Highland Light Infantry, recalled this novel way of entering the battle zone:

"Zero hour was at 5.30 A.M. as I have said, but it was earlier than that when we commenced to move from the cellars to the front. The first part of our subterranean journey was very slow, as we could only proceed in single file through the narrow and torturous passages that had been constructed from cellar to cellar, but when we reached the main sewer the going was easier, though still slow and in single file. Many jokes were passed among the men as we made our way along that salubrious emergency thoroughfare. In the good old days troops went into battle with colours flying and bands playing, but there is not much romance in advancing to the attack through a city sewer!"

From AND ALL FOR WHAT? SOME WAR TIME EXPERIENCES *by D. W. J. Cuddeford (Heath Cranton, 1933).*

Canadian recruiting poster of World War I. *The great victory of the Canadian Corps at Vimy Ridge significantly raised Canadian morale.*

ZERO HOUR

On the day of attack, the British were further helped by a downpour of rain turning to snow, obscuring their advance from the enemy. Covered by a creeping barrage, British and Imperial troops advanced rapidly across no-man's-land. German artillery was surprisingly quiet, thanks to gas shells having killed the horses that should have kept them supplied with ammunition.

The surprise of the attack was recalled by B. Neyland, a radio operator in the Royal Engineers: "4 A.M. The barrage opened with a mighty roar and there it fell incessantly just across the waste. 'Go!' Over the top we clambered, over the stricken wilderness we stumbled. We wireless 'merchants' mixed with the infantry, hoping for some protection. We carried no bayonets, our unloaded rifles were strapped across our backs and our only means of defence was apparently fists. Why wireless operators were not allowed to load their rifles we never learned. We attained the enemy lines. Jerry was engaged in peaceful

RIGHT *A German soldier observes Allied advances* *through a periscope which enables him to look over the edge of his trench without being shot by snipers. He holds a hand grenade and wears the new stalhelm antishrapnel helmet.*

BELOW *British machine-gun team wearing gas masks.* *Poison gas was employed effectively in the initial British attack on the German line at Arras.*

domestic functions! Some washing, others making coffee, and many had to be awakened to be taken captive. The blow had fallen before they expected it."

In under an hour, the entire German front line east of Arras was taken. The Canadian Corps, attacking with its four divisions side by side, surged over Vimy Ridge to the north of Arras, strategically important high ground that had defied Allied attack for almost three years. It was a legendary victory that enormously raised Canadian morale.

Allenby's Third Army made excellent progress east of Arras, helped partly by new and effective artillery shells. The Ninth and Fourth Divisions made a leapfrog advance of more than 6,000 yards, representing a record penetration of the enemy line for the whole war so far. And all this was achieved with minimum casualties. It showed the way the war should have been fought.

Unfortunately, the British did not realize the extent to which they had damaged the Germans. By the next day the great advantage had been partially lost, as the Germans resumed their defense with more ferocity. The British attacks faltered and the great breakthrough was not achieved.

LEFT ***German medical orderly tends a wounded British soldier.*** *Both sides acted relatively humanely toward each other but, in the heat of battle, many surrendering soldiers were killed, especially machine gunners who had just killed dozens of attacking soldiers.*

VIMY RIDGE

General Edmund Allenby *was the commander of Allied forces at the battle of Arras and Vimy Ridge. He was a competent general, who made the most of recent developments in tactics and weapons to achieve an impressive victory.*

In 1917 Arras was a city of ruins, with many of its citizens confined to living in the cellars and tunnels beneath it. Today the French city has been rebuilt and makes a useful base for exploring the surrounding remnants of the Western Front.

To its north, Vimy Ridge possesses one of the most interesting memorials to the soldiers of World War I. The twin pillars of the Canadian Memorial rise high above the wooded slopes of Hill 145. The shell-cratered, 240-acre Memorial Park it overlooks has been preserved by the Canadian government and was a gift from the French government. In the park, one can see the opposing trenches of both the German and Canadian front lines.

There is a myriad of tunnels beneath the surface of the park. Between October 1916 and March 1917 over six miles of tunnels were dug by the Allies and the Germans, all of it lit by electricity. Inside the tunnels were operational headquarters, dressing stations, an ammunition store, and accommodation for the soldiers. Even narrow-gauge railways were laid. They were resistant to bombardment, and ventilation shafts provided adequate air supply.

Although the victories at Vimy Ridge and Arras were a success for the British and Canadian armies, there were still a great many casualties. German counterattacks were fierce and the speed of the advance could bring its own dangers, as Lieutenant Cuddeford remembered: "Something of a surprise awaited as we pushed on over Observation Ridge, for there on the reverse slope, not more than two to three hundred yards directly in front of us, were two batteries of German field guns that opened point-blank fire on us as soon as we appeared in view…in the few minutes we were under that deadly fire several men were killed and a number terribly wounded."

PLAN OF BATTLE

On April 9, 1917, the British Third Army under Allenby attacked east of Arras against the German Sixth Army and advanced as far as Bailleul, Fampoux, and Monchy. Four divisions of the Canadian Corps attacked Vimy Ridge and one Bavarian Reserve Corps to the north of Arras and captured it along with 4,000 prisoners, fifty-four artillery guns, 105 mortars, and 125 machine guns. In total the Allies captured 13,000 German prisoners and some 200 artillery guns.

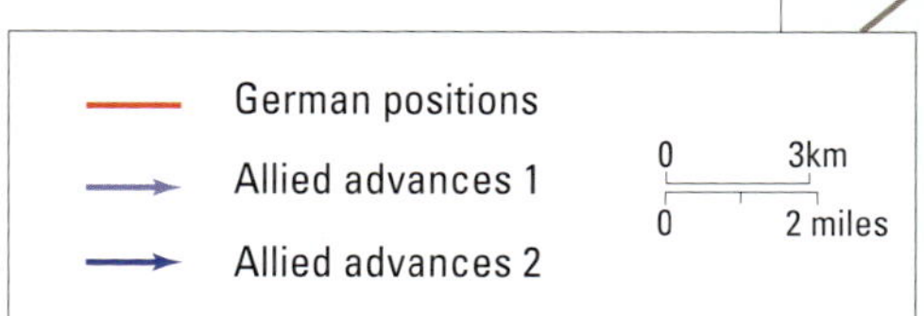

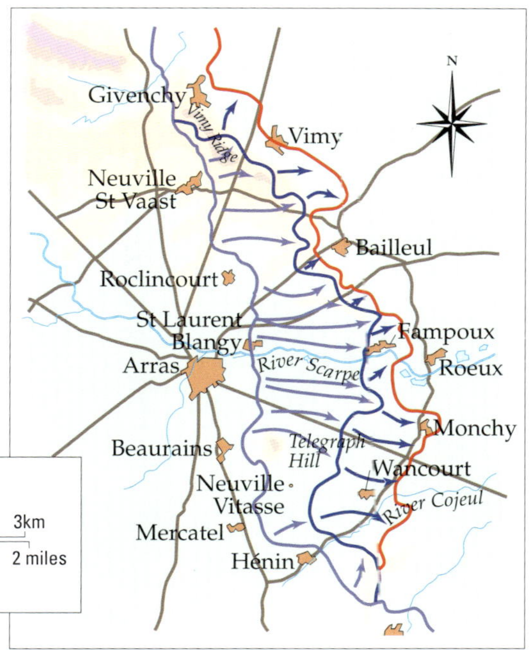

VIMY RIDGE

THE CANADIAN MEMORIAL PARK on Vimy Ridge is a beautifully preserved section of the Western Front with trenches and tunnels to visit alongside memorials. Although visitors are very welcome, it must be remembered that the entire park is a memorial, and picnics and games are not allowed among the shell craters. Wired-off sections of the park should not be visited, as unexploded bombs and mines are still there.

ABOVE *German concrete gun* *emplacement near Givenchy.*

GETTING THERE

LOCATION: *Between Arras and Lens, northern France.*

VISITOR INORMATION: *French Tourist Office, Hotel de Ville, Place des Heros, 62000 Arras.*

TELEPHONE: *03 3 2151 2695*

DIRECTIONS: *By road, from Lens take C26 autoroute southeast toward Arras. At Vimy-Givenchy crossroads follow D51 toward Givenchy and on to Canadian Memorial Park.*

TOUR DISTANCE: *1 mile (1.6km).*

CANADIAN MEMORIAL

This memorial (2) rises high above the slopes of Hill 145. Good views of the surrounding battle-scarred landscape add to the appreciation of history.

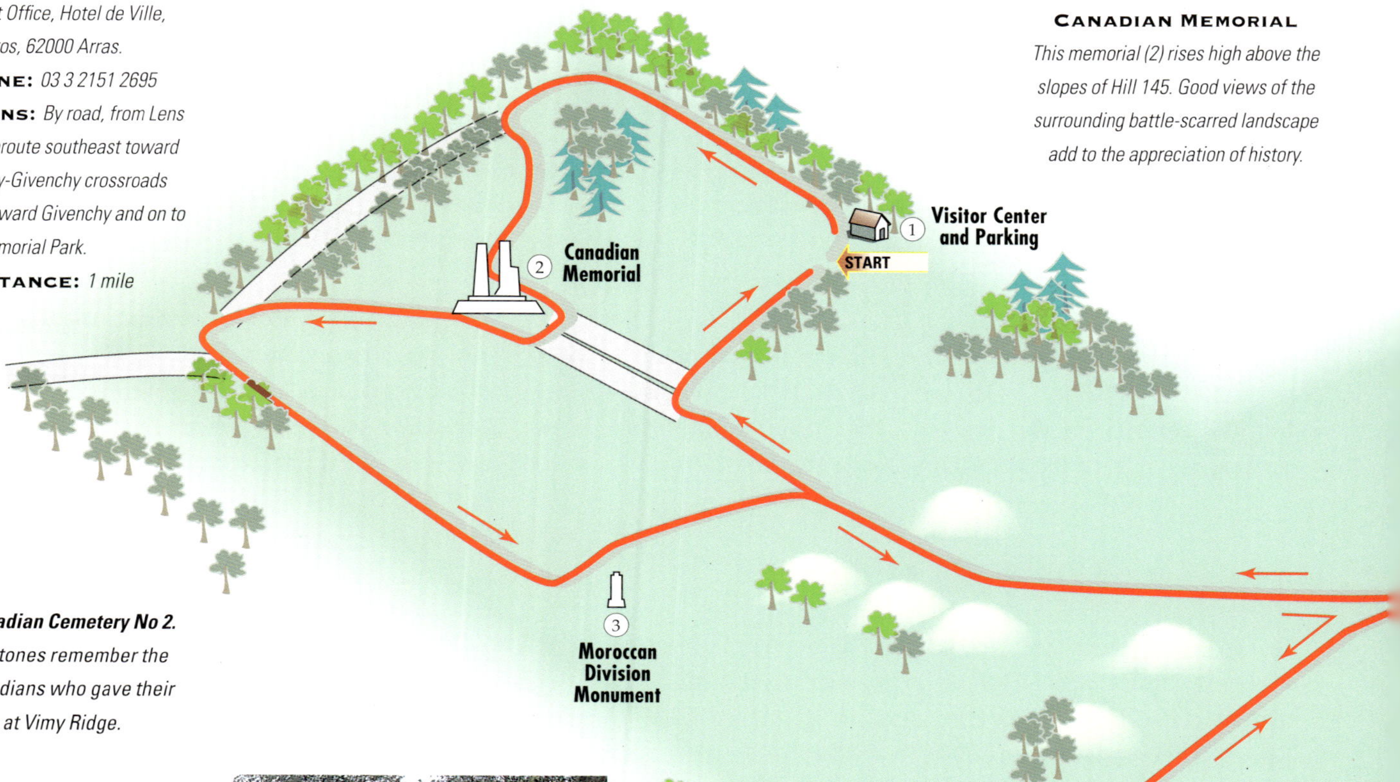

BELOW *Canadian Cemetery No 2.* *Ranks of stones remember the many Canadians who gave their lives at Vimy Ridge.*

LEFT *Shell-cratered Memorial Park* *has been preserved by the Canadian government.*

RIGHT *Restored German trenches* *(7) near Grange Tunnel, represent the front line position.*

CANADIAN AND GERMAN FRONT-LINE TRENCHES

Well preserved with concrete sandbags and duckboards (7). At the rear of the German front line is a pillbox and trench mortar. From the Canadian front line runs a short section of the supporting trench left in its natural state.

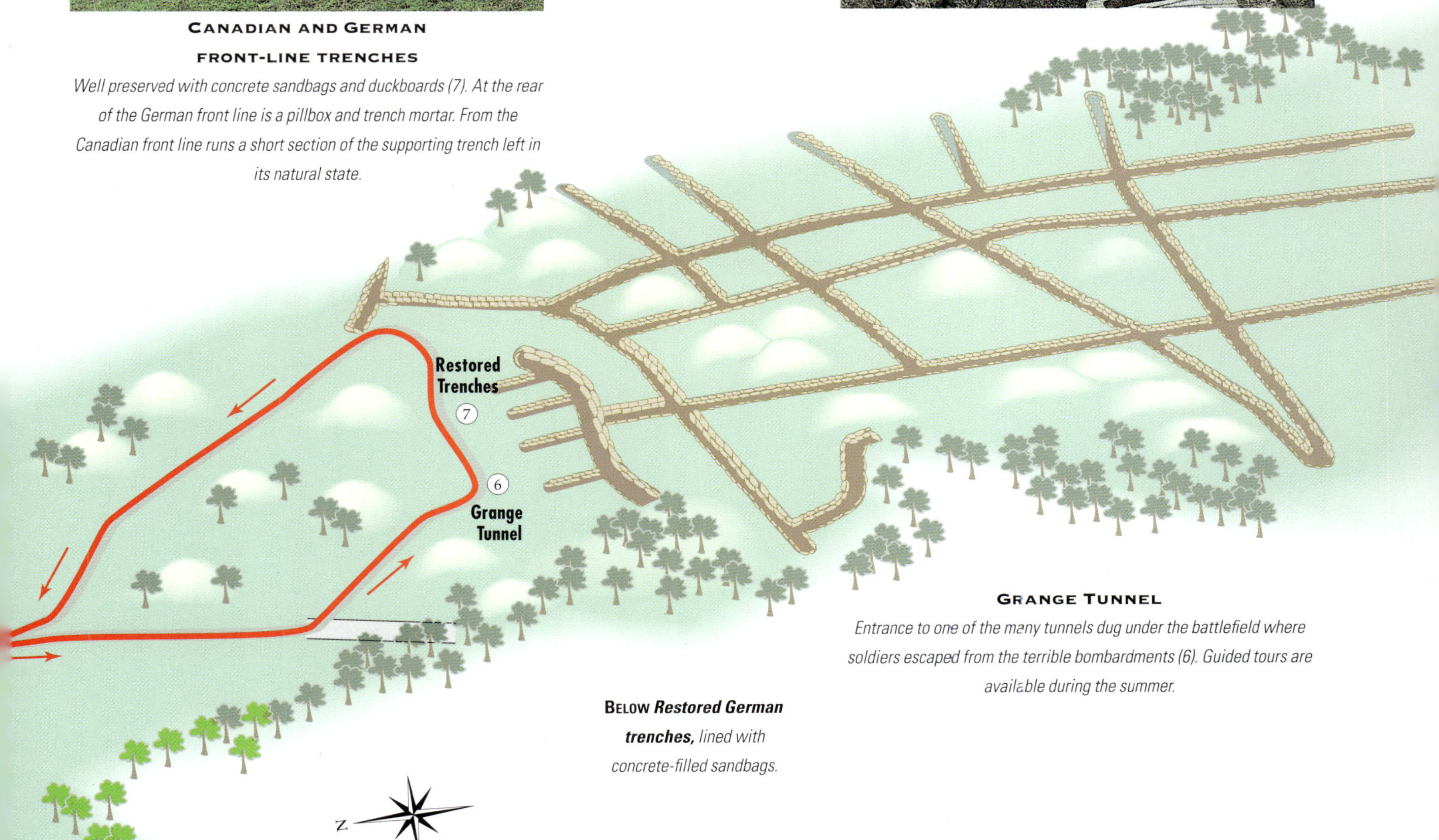

GRANGE TUNNEL

Entrance to one of the many tunnels dug under the battlefield where soldiers escaped from the terrible bombardments (6). Guided tours are available during the summer.

BELOW *Restored German trenches,* *lined with concrete-filled sandbags.*

POLISH RESISTANCE

Above *Double fencing of barbed wire* *and a watchtower guard the edge of Majdanek Concentration Camp near Lublin, the final destination for many Poles and Jews from Warsaw. Some 360,000 were killed either by mass shootings or in gas chambers.*

Left *German war leader Adolf Hitler* *watches his troops march into Poland. Despite stiff resistance, Poland fell to German aggression within a month and had to endure six years of brutal occupation.*

Warsaw was one of the first great casualties of World War II. The beautiful capital of Poland, rich in eighteenth- and nineteenth-century architecture and with a multicultural population including almost 500,000 Jews, was one of the first great cities of Europe to feel the full force of German aggression. On September 1, 1939 Germany invaded Poland. Armored columns and aircraft pulverized the Polish army and, despite bitter resistance, reached the Polish capital on September 16. "The Poles were effectively a World War I force fighting a World War II war," concludes Major Nick Bunday, a British army battlefield guide in Poland. "The entire Polish defense budget in 1939 equated to a mere ten percent of the *Luftwaffe* budget alone!"

Warsaw refused to surrender and faced ten days of saturation bombing before it was forced to capitulate. Many of its buildings had been destroyed and the population traumatized by days without food and water. The mayor estimated that some 40,000 citizens died in this first assault on their capital. More bad news followed when the Soviet army invaded eastern Poland in an agreed division of the country resulting from the Nazi-Soviet Pact. For Warsaw, the nightmare had only just begun.

BACKGROUND TO BATTLE

The circumstances of the Warsaw Uprising in 1944 have long been blamed upon Stalin and his cynical desire to see the forces of Polish nationalism destroyed by the Germans before the Communists took over the city. Stalin would certainly not have wept over the death of anti-Soviet Poles, but it seems that the Polish warriors in Warsaw truly miscalculated the help the Soviet army could lend them. They believed too readily Soviet radio broadcasts that spoke of imminent liberty, for the Red Army was not able to easily enter Warsaw or give military assistance. They were meeting stiff German resistance, and Soviet generals on the front line concluded there was little they could do to push forward.

There is a further twist to the events in Warsaw—the Polish Home Army consisted mainly of nationalists who were against Communist domination. They did not want to see the Soviet army enter Warsaw before they could liberate it themselves. It seems therefore that the uprising was timed in the hope of winning the city for themselves just before the Soviets appeared on the scene, thus strengthening their grasp on their own capital. Tragically, they miscalculated the strength of both the German and Russian armies.

JEWISH SUFFERING

Warsaw was now under the brutal rule of the German Gestapo and SS, and their principal target of oppression was its large Jewish population. All Jews were gathered and forced to live in a small area of less than two and a half miles (four square kilometers) in the center of the city known as the Warsaw Ghetto. "The site of the ghetto was probably chosen for purely logistical reasons since it was near a railhead," says Professor Felix Tych, director of the Jewish Institute in Poland. "The Nazis attempted a 'hermetic seal' but food still got through and the guards could be bribed." In July 1942, 6,000 Jews a day were deported in trains to extermination camps in the east, such as Treblinka and Majdanek.

One camp worker managed to escape from Treblinka and returned to Warsaw to warn the Jews of their fate. "It was when the ghetto inmates heard of a plan to remove them all to the gas chambers that they rebelled," recalls Professor Tych, who is one of the few Jews to have survived this period. "The Nazis

ABOVE *Monument to the victims of the Warsaw Ghetto,* *commemorating the half-million Warsaw Jews who were exterminated by the Germans.*

LEFT *Polish prisoners of war.* *Many Poles escaped abroad and fought in the Allied forces as pilots or soldiers during the Allied invasion of Europe. Some Polish men formed the core of resistance that would rise as the Home Army in Warsaw in 1944.*

responded by torching the houses, throwing grenades into the cellars and shooting anyone who came out. I saw it with my own eyes."

The Jewish underground gathered weapons to make a stand and, on April 19, 1943, a 1,200-strong army of Jews opened fire on German soldiers who were marching into the ghetto to finish off the remaining Jews. For almost a month, they fought heroically against overwhelming odds until the Germans bombed and burned the ghetto to rubble. The Synagogue was blown up on May 16, the eve of Passover. Some 7,000 Jews died in the battle and over 56,000 were transported to Treblinka.

Although not victim to the systematic extermination of the Jews, the rest of the population of Warsaw suffered daily from the cruelties of a German government who considered Slavic Poles to be an inferior race. When the war turned against the Germans in the east and the Soviet army began to push them back to Poland, the Poles of Warsaw dreamed of their imminent freedom. Soviet radio broadcasts encouraged this feeling and, on July 29, 1944, came the message: "People of Warsaw, to arms! Attack the Germans! Help the Red Army."

The Polish government in exile in London gave permission to the Polish Home Army, or Armija Krajowa (A.K.), to launch an insurrection against the Germans.

WARSAW HORROR

Armed mainly with weapons captured from the Germans, some 40,000 A.K. soldiers under the command of Major General Tadeusz Bor-Komorowski rose on August 1. Homemade bombs and mines exploded around the city and Germans came under fire from snipers. German garrisons were overrun, and three-fifths of the city fell into Polish hands, but they failed to capture the railway stations or bridges over the Vistula. Most importantly, the Soviet army was nowhere close to entering the city and a German counterattack forced the Red Army back about sixty miles (100 kilometers).

German reinforcements poured into the city of Warsaw and, under the leadership of

BACKGROUND ***German machine gun crew*** *on the outskirts of Warsaw in September 1939.*

ESCAPE FROM HELL

Aside from the Polish Home Army, surviving Jewish resistance fighters from the Warsaw Ghetto battle, civilian men, women, and children were all caught up in the bitter fighting during the Warsaw Uprising and the German assault that followed. One Warsaw woman, Krystyna Szelinska, kept a diary of her feelings during the battle:

"Escape from the fighting is a nightmare. On the way we pass wounded soldiers and can't take them all with us. Fear grabs our throats and I feel scared above all else. I just want to run without looking away from this hell. Finally, we get to Kazimierzowska Street. We run to a place and just fall asleep. From early on in the morning there is fighting two streets away and one street is blocked by Germans. I cannot stand anymore the whining sound of Stuka dive-bombers and cover my head. I am losing my nerve, going mad. Janka is shot in the leg, but not seriously. She can still walk. Kora orders us to evacuate and gives us passes to show when we enter the sewers. I am frightened to death about going down the sewers, but I am more frightened of the Germans."

Quoted in DWA WRZESNIE *by Halina Krahelska, translated by Monika Brzozowska (Warsaw, 1983).*

Junkers Ju-87 Stuka dive-bomber, *chief aerial terror weapon used by the Germans during the Warsaw Uprising.*

SS Lt. Gen. Erich von dem Bach-Zelewski, they unleashed a brutal campaign of annihilation against the Polish rebels. Awesome weapons were brought to bear on the Poles, including a giant 4,800-pound mortar called "Karl", and minitanks packed with explosives called "Goliaths", as well as a railborne giant gun, Junkers Ju-87 Stuka dive-bombers, and flame-throwers.

Resistance centered on the Old Town, a knot of medieval streets surrounded by old castle walls. Noncombatants huddled in the cellars of their homes while Polish men, women, and children fought bitterly for every street and building. Little girls used the sewers to deliver messages to the fighters, despite Germans placing barbed wire down them. The populace bravely defended their homes. Against them were the very worst the Nazi regime could recruit: professional murderers, including 4,000 armed criminals from a penal brigade, as well as brutalized veterans from the eastern front. They massacred, burned, and raped any Poles that fell into their hands. "On Hitler's direct orders the Nazi soldiers behaved barbarically," says Professor Andrzej Ajnenkiel, director of the Polish Military Historical Institute. "Warsaw was completely destroyed and her citizens murdered, including small children." Doctors and nurses were shot; hospital patients were burned alive; and prisoners were used as human shields in front of German tanks.

The Soviet army could see the smoke rising above Warsaw, but did little to help the Poles inside the city. Many Poles thought they were doing this on purpose, letting the Germans destroy the bravest of the defenders to make it easier for the Russians to eventually control their capital. The Western Allies dropped a few supplies onto the city, but that was the most they could achieve. Polish troops in the Red Army launched an attack on the city in September but were so little trusted by the nationalist Poles inside that the attacks were not coordinated and had little impact.

Hunger, disease, and a lack of supplies now began to undermine the courage of the Poles in the Old Town and, on October 2, they had to accept that there would be no outside help. They were forced to surrender and, surprisingly, the Germans granted the remaining fighters prisoner-of-war status. Some 200,000 Warsaw civilians and 15,000 A.K. soldiers died in the inferno, but they had inflicted 26,000 casualties on the Germans, including 10,000 dead. The Old Town was utterly demolished. A bitter lesson was learned by the Poles which would haunt them in later years, as Professor Jan Ciechanowski explains: "We learned from the uprising that one should seek independence by peaceful means when faced with overwhelming odds. If Poland had risen against the Russians, like Hungary in 1956, it would have been a calamity. You could say that for Poland, World War II ended with our independence in 1989."

ABOVE *The Old Town* *in Warsaw has been meticulously restored brick by brick, building by building, since it was completely destroyed by the German army during World War II.*

WARSAW OLD TOWN

THE OLD TOWN lies at the heart of Warsaw, being its oldest and most charming area, full of winding cobbled streets, elegant merchant houses, and a vibrant square lined with restaurants. It is hard to believe that this picturesque quarter of Warsaw witnessed the most bitter and horrific fighting of the Warsaw Uprising in 1944. More than 100,000 citizens were crammed in the cellars of these antique houses while the men, women, and children of the Home Army fought for every building as the Germans ruthlessly closed in on them.

It is even harder to believe that all the buildings of the Old Town were demolished by the Germans after the surrender of its defenders, leaving just piles of rubble. But as soon as the war was over and Germany defeated, the citizens of Warsaw rebuilt every building in the Old Town until it resembled exactly its former glory. What you see all around you now in the Old Town is the result of this heroic effort to defy the destruction of the war and demonstrate the indomitable Polish spirit. Emblematic of this process is the church in the Old Town, which was demolished by a Goliath. After the war, the church was completely reconstructed, and the tracks of the tank bomb that destroyed it are now incorporated into the side of the rebuilt church.

Monument to the thousands of children

who fought and died in the Warsaw Uprising, situated in the battlements of the Old Town.

The area of the Warsaw Ghetto, near the Old Town, has not been totally reconstructed. At the heart of the pitifully small space that once housed some half a million Jews is now a square with grass covering land that formed the final standing place of Warsaw's Jewish population. A fine monument commemorates their suffering and sacrifice.

PLAN OF BATTLE

Although the Warsaw Uprising in 1944 took place throughout the city, the German counterattack forced the Polish Home Army to consolidate its resistance around the Old Town on the banks of the Vistula. Sewers proved a useful means of communication under the devastated streets. German forces attacked from the west, fighting with the Polish Home Army for every street. After the remaining Poles surrendered, the entire Old Town was demolished.

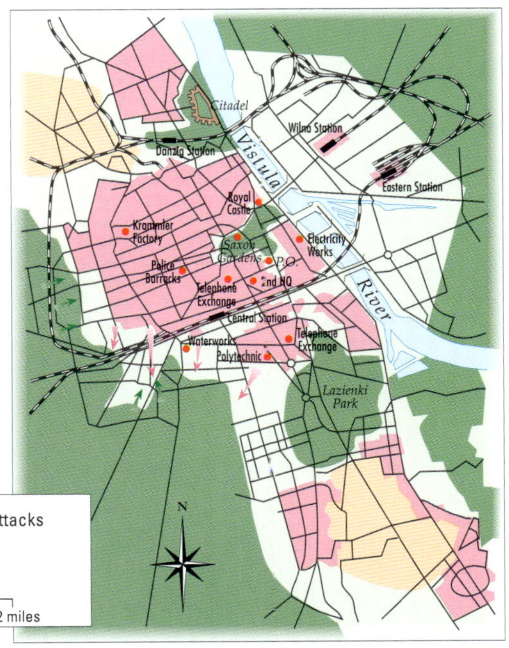

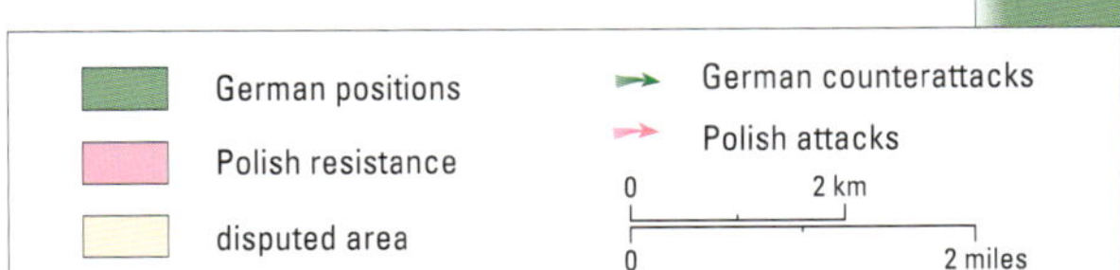

WARSAW

WARSAW HAS EMERGED from the Cold War era as a dynamic city with the Old Town as its attractive, popular heart. Walking along its charming cobbled streets between restaurants and busy bars, it is difficult to imagine the devastation that faced its citizens just over half a century ago.

ABOVE *Members of a British army* *battlefield tour examine the graves of Polish Home Army soldiers who died during the Warsaw Uprising.*

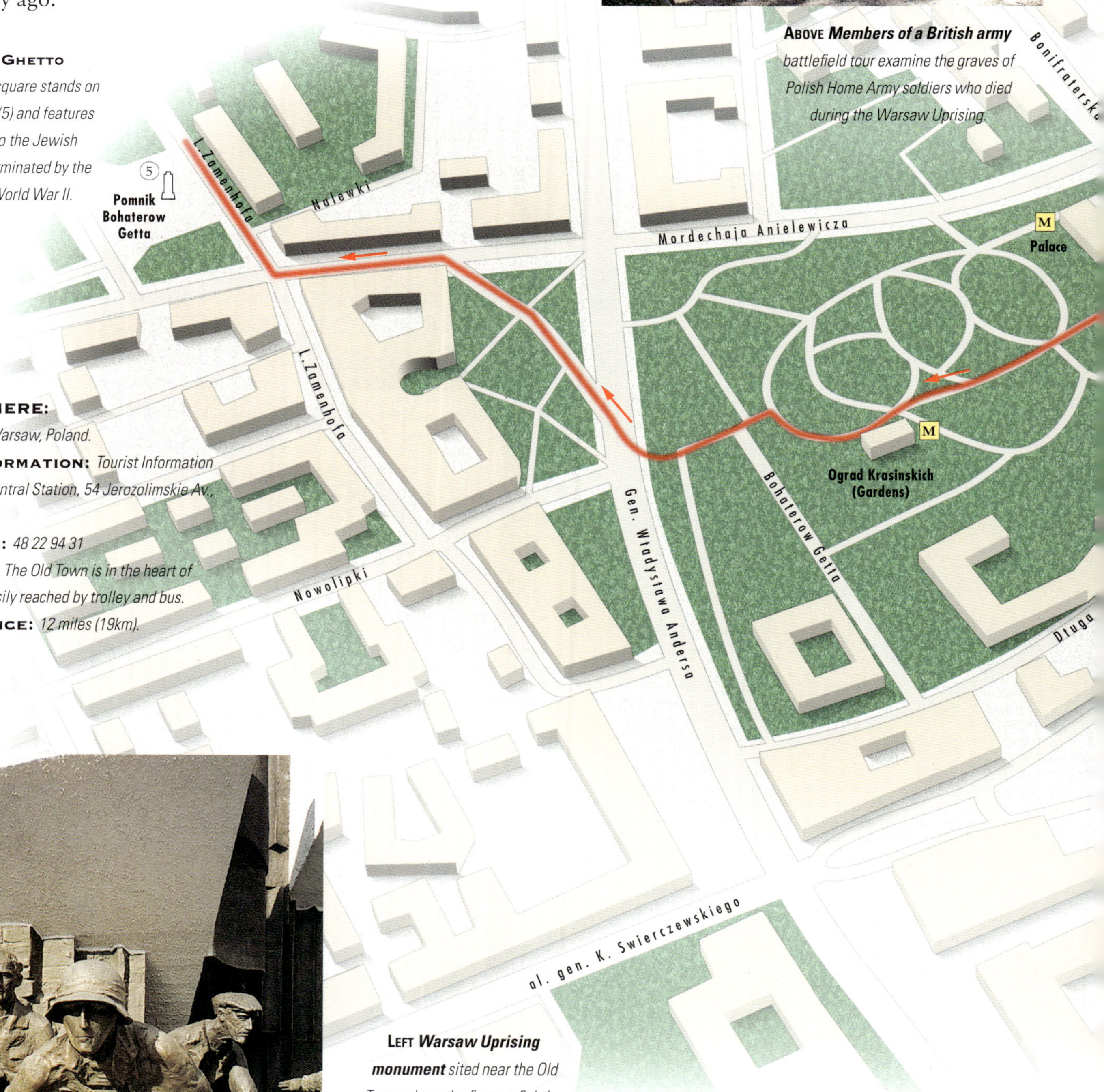

WARSAW GHETTO

A grass-covered square stands on part of this area (5) and features a monument to the Jewish population exterminated by the Germans in World War II.

GETTING THERE:

LOCATION: *Warsaw, Poland.*

VISITOR INFORMATION: *Tourist Information Office, Warsaw Central Station, 54 Jerozolimskie Av., 00-024, Warsaw.*

TELEPHONE: *48 22 94 31*

DIRECTIONS: *The Old Town is in the heart of Warsaw and is easily reached by trolley and bus.*

TOUR DISTANCE: *12 miles (19km).*

LEFT *Warsaw Uprising monument* *sited near the Old Town where the fiercest fighting took place as the Germans closed in on the defenders. Monument designed by W. Kuema and J. Budyn.*

Krasinski Square

Warsaw Uprising Monument (4), erected in 1989, vividly depicts some of its defenders equipped with captured German equipment.

Old Town

The main square of the Old Town (1) marks the core of the area to which the Polish Home Army retreated to defend at the height of the Warsaw Uprising.

Above ***Dramatic section of the Warsaw Uprising*** *monument raised in 1989, showing the Home Army wearing stolen German helmets and fighting with captured guns.*

Church of Archikatedra

In the side of this church (2) in the Old Town are embedded the tracks of the minitank bomb that destroyed the building in 1944.

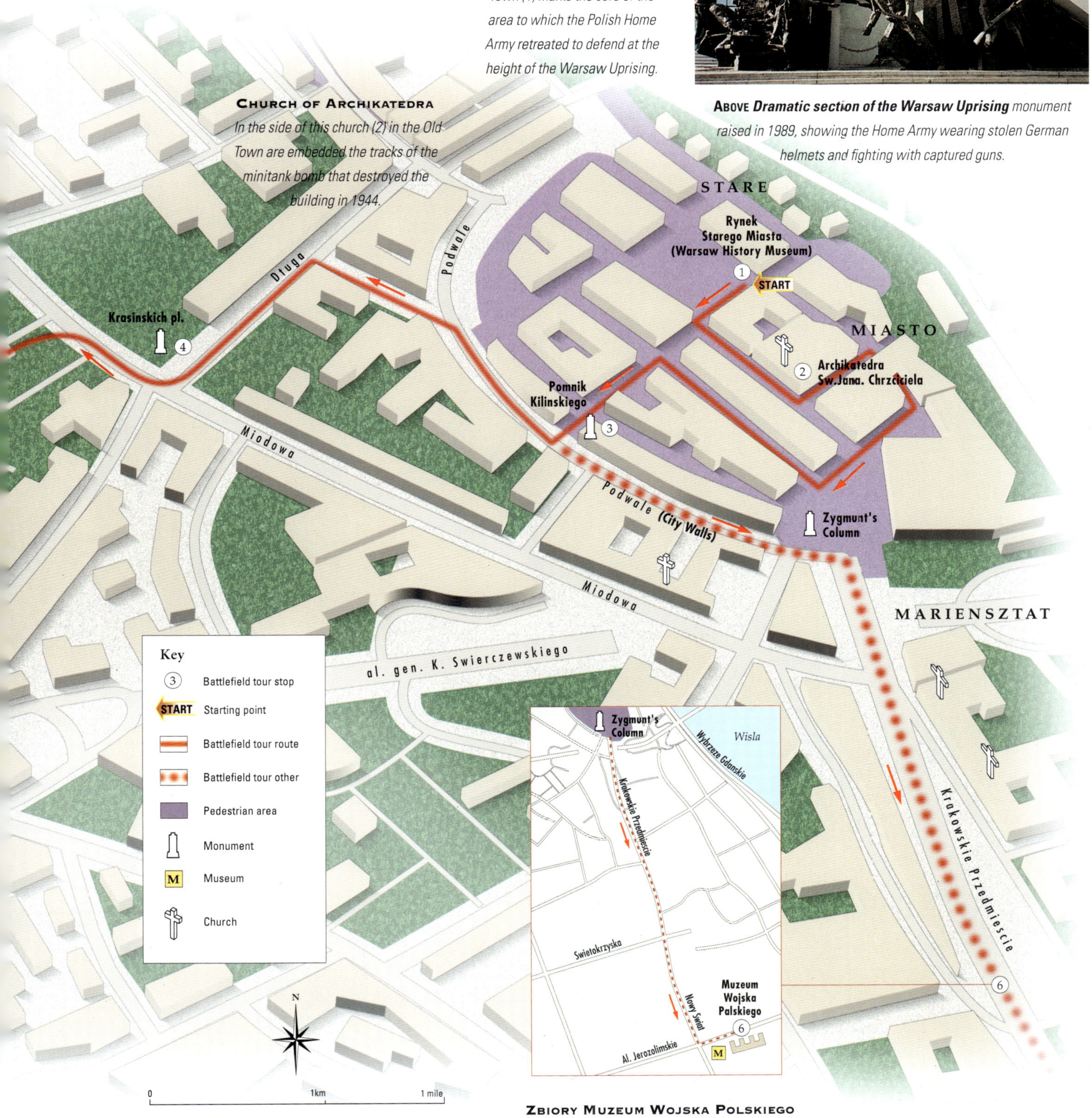

Zbiory Muzeum Wojska Polskiego

Polish Military Museum (6) tells the entire story of the Polish army, with many rooms devoted to World War II. There are outdoor military vehicle exhibits as well.

BATTLE OF BRITAIN

ABOVE ***Defiant British poster*** *warning of the danger of incendiary bombs dropped during German air raids.*

LEFT ***London firemen fighting to save a blazing warehouse*** *during the Blitz. Many air attacks occurred at night.*

ADOLF HITLER, THE GERMAN NAZI LEADER, always had ambivalent feelings about his great wartime foe, Britain. On the one hand, he admired Britain's empire greatly and saw the nation as a fellow Germanic race with whom he might jointly rule the world; but on the other, he hated Britain's implacable resistance to his plans in Europe and wanted to see it defeated. Eventually he was persuaded by Hermann Goering, commander of the German air force, the *Luftwaffe*, that Britain could be defeated in the air, leaving the opportunity open for an invasion of the country. The great struggle between the two air forces began in the summer of 1940 and became known as the Battle of Britain.

TERROR CAMPAIGN

In August 1940 the first massive air assault began on Britain. For ten days, some 900 German fighter planes and 1,300 bombers flew over 1,000 sorties against English air bases and ports, day and night. The plan was to annihilate Britain's ability to defend itself and, if the combat was

BACKGROUND TO BATTLE

The Blitz was not the first time Londoners had come under attack from above. On January 15, 1915, during World War I, a series of giant rigid airships called Zeppelins appeared over Britain and dropped bombs on civilian targets. It was the first of many such raids. "I remember one bad one in Leicester Square [in London]," recalled Margaret Warren, a nurse. "I had been there the week before and had a marvelous time. The week after that the whole place was bombed to small pieces. Some Zeppelin had come along and bumped them off. Several of my friends were there, which was very sad. That rather shook me." In total, some 196 tons of bombs were dropped and 557 people were killed.

Although the Zeppelin raids were never a major threat, the concept had been evolved and by World War II, long-range bomber aircraft had been developed which could threaten all major cities in Europe. The German air force began its use of bombing raids during the Spanish Civil War, when it devastated the town of Guernica. By 1939, when the Germans invaded Poland and then western Europe, bomber aircraft were a vital part of the combined arms assault on enemy, military, and civilian targets. This form of attack became known as the blitzkrieg (lightning war), from which the British took the name Blitz for their own experience of this brutal form of warfare.

to be decided on numbers, then Germany held the upper hand. The *Luftwaffe* planes outnumbered the British R.A.F. almost four to one, with Britain only able to muster 650 planes, although these did include the legendary Supermarine Spitfire and Hawker Hurricane, superior fighter aircraft that the Germans came to fear. Although the German Messerschmitt Me-109E was a match for either British fighter, its limited range, which allowed only about twenty minutes of loiter time over England, put its pilots at a disadvantage. In addition to this, Britain possessed radar, which gave British air bases advanced warning of German air attacks.

The first attack failed to break Britain's defenses, but a second massive assault came at the end of August and ran into September 1940. Groups of bombers, escorted by fighters, devastated major R.A.F. bases, destroying some

KIEL BOMBED FROM 800 FEET: BACK PAGE

H-P SAUCE IMPROVES TASTE STOPS WASTE

Daily Sketch

Tastes Lovely! BROWN & POLSON Custard

R.A.F. Repulse Waves Of Bombers, Shoot Down 24 (at least)

NAZIS RAID LONDON —AND 13 TOWNS

HE CAN'T KEEP AWAY FROM HIS JOB

Mr. Churchill Sees Coast Battles

After successive waves of German raiders, concentrating on South-East England, had failed to break through the R.A.F.'s fighter defences yesterday. Nazi bombers renewed their wide-spread night raids throughout the country, and the London area experienced its fifth successive night alarm.

'Keep Your Pecker Up

Adopting the "nuisance" tactics of the previous nights, enemy aircraft approached the London area singly, were picked up in the searchlights and "ushered" away from the Metropolis.

Shortly after the sirens stopped a group of parachute flares dropped over one suburb far out.

Mr. Churchill saw some of the fiercest air fights of the war when he visited the South-East coast.

He watched the aerial battles over Dover and inspected the wreckage of a Messerschmitt which crashed in flames.

CONTINUED ON BACK PAGE.

FACING HOME, THAT'S AS FAR AS HE GOT!

RIGHT Londoners sleep on the platform *of an underground train station to escape the bombing above.*

LEFT Front page of a contemporary British newspaper *reporting the Blitz in August 1940.*

THE KING STAMMERS

The Blitz was a terrifying experience for parents and older people, but children were less aware of the danger and frequently saw it as an excuse not to go to school. Peter Newark, a schoolboy living to the east of London during the Blitz, remembered seeing the Battle of Britain at first hand in the sky above his home:

"A Messerschmitt 109, a German fighter plane, flew down my street, just above the houses and shot up the gas storage tower at the end of the road. Fortunately, it didn't explode, as it would have taken the street with it, but I rushed inside and told my Dad. 'D-d-d-d-dad,' I said, stammering badly, and he said 'stop stammering.' So, quick as a flash, I said, 'well the King stammers,' which he did [George VI] and my Dad gave me a clip round the head which I thought was a bit rich, considering what I'd just seen and what we'd just survived."

Quoted in WAR IN BRITAIN *by Tim Newark (HarperCollins, 2000).*

A German pilot gets ready *to fly his Messerschmitt Me-109E as an escort for the vast armadas of bombers that attacked Britain during the Blitz.*

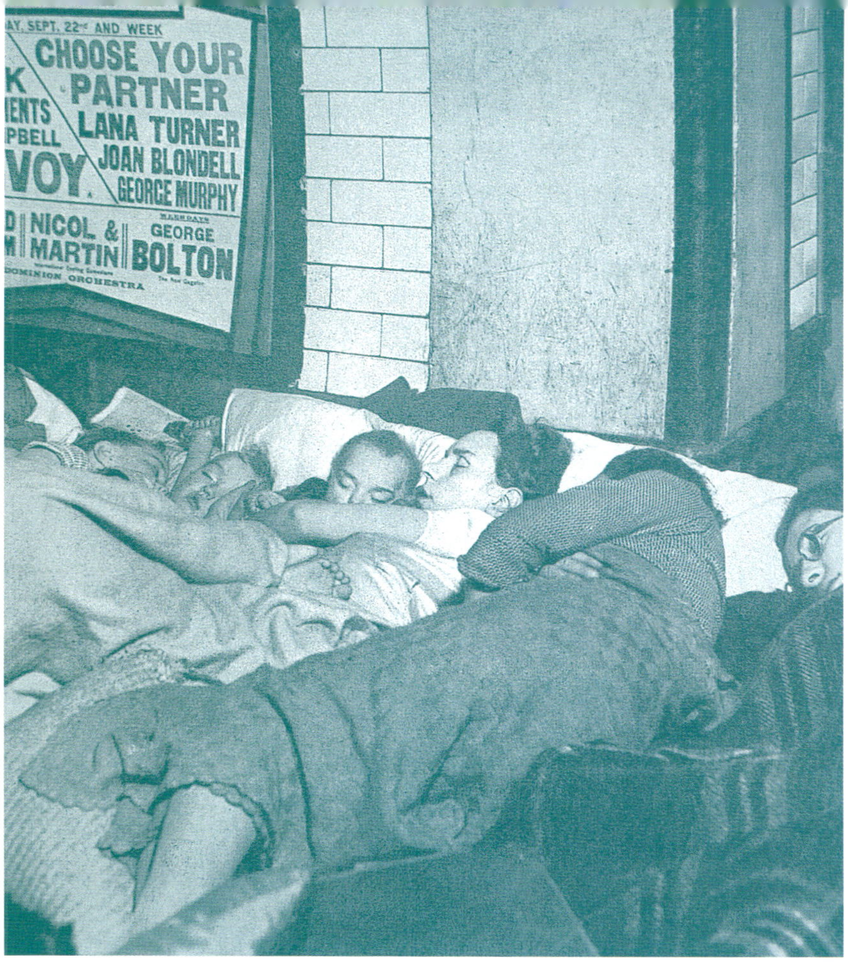

450 British fighter planes. On the edge of defeat, Britain responded by launching its first bombing raids on German cities. Infuriated, Hitler now instructed Göering to shift his assault from military targets to civilian targets. Ordinary residents of Britain were now on the front line and experienced the terror of total war. But the shift in targets helped give the R.A.F. a space to reconstruct its strength and renew its defense of the country.

The Blitz had begun, and London experienced its full fury from September 7 to the end of the month. On one day, September 15, more than 1,000 German bombers and 700 fighter planes flew over the capital, killing hundreds of civilians and reducing many of its historic buildings to rubble. As the principal targets for Germany's terror raids, London and its citizens quickly had to learn to protect themselves. Thousands volunteered to join the A.R.P. (Air Raid Precautions) and A.F.S. (Auxiliary Fire Service).

Public air-raid shelters were constructed throughout the city. Basements in buildings were converted for public use, and Anderson shelters, consisting of a hole in the ground covered with a piece of corrugated iron, were erected in back gardens. Primitive defenses, they were useless against direct hits and frequently filled with rainwater, prompting one crowd of women to mount a protest, holding placards complaining "Sink or swim in Romford shelters" and "Is pneumonia better than bombs?"

PUT THAT LIGHT OUT!

As the bombing of London continued, underground train stations provided the safest deep shelters and were equipped with 200,000 bunks as well as stoves and sanitation. Enterprising people started little lending libraries on the station platforms and a tube train provided food from station to station. The blackout became a regular occurrence, in which all lights were extinguished at night so as not to provide bombers above with any targets. It was the job of the white-helmeted A.R.P. wardens to ensure that this was carried out and their cry of "Put that light out!" became a much-disliked irritation at the time. Sometimes the blackout itself caused casualties. Familiar streets became hazardous obstacles in complete darkness, and there were numerous fatal accidents. Some

BELOW *Soldiers delicately remove an unexploded 1200- pound German bomb* *dropped in September 1940. One in ten bombs dropped on London failed to explode, and some are still uncovered today.*

ABOVE *Winston Churchill,* *British Prime Minister during the Blitz, embodied the defiant spirit of the British people at this testing time. (Painting by Douglas Chandor.)*

responded to the blackout difficulties with ingenuity, such as the woman who supplied luminous paint for keyholes.

The way to hit back at the bombers was with a network of active air defenses such as antiaircraft guns and searchlights. Women became involved as crews for these antiaircraft guns, and it was one of the few ways they could actively engage the enemy. Forming defensive lines on either side of the Thames, these AA guns could throw up ten shells a minute to 41,000 feet. Despite this, few aircraft were actually shot down, and the AA guns acted more as morale boosters, sometimes deterring bombers from attacking particular areas, but then they would simply drop their bombs elsewhere. Barrage balloons were another idea, rising above London to create a mesh of obstacles with their long cables hindering low-flying fighters.

The best defense for London and other British cities remained the R.A.F., and on that brutal day of September 15, it shot down fifty-six German aircraft for a loss of twenty-six of its own. The tide was beginning to turn. British bombers destroyed part of the invasion fleet gathered on the continent, and Hitler finally decided to call off his invasion plans. The Battle of Britain was won, and the British Prime Minister, Winston Churchill, gave public thanks to the R.A.F., when he said: "Never, in the field of human conflict, was so much owed by so many to so few." Some 915 British aircraft had been shot down, but they had accounted for almost twice as many enemy planes. Invasion no longer threatened Britain, but a vengeful Hitler continued to order bombing raids over London and other British cities simply to terrorize the population.

On the night of November 14, 1940, the city of Coventry was attacked by 500 German bombers and virtually wiped out. The German air assault on Britain killed more than 43,000 men, women, and children in or near their homes, and badly injured an additional 50,000. It was the worst attack ever experienced by Britain's civilian population. The worst of the Blitz came to an end in May 1941 as Hitler shifted his main military interest toward Russia, but the bombing of London continued, and in the summer of 1944 came a further shock.

Thinking that the war was coming to an end, Londoners were then assaulted by German missiles called V–1s and V–2s. Arriving without warning, these proved devastating. More than 2,000 V–1 flying bombs and 1,000 V–2 missiles were launched against Britain, destroying more than 30,000 houses and damaging 1.25 million in London alone. Only when Allied troops overran their launch sites in Europe did the misery of the Blitz finally come to an end.

BACKGROUND *Barrage balloons rose above London* *during the Blitz,as a means of hindering low-flying attacks by German aircraft.*

LEFT *Badges of Britain's Civil Defence* *organizations during the Blitz.*

LONDON BLITZ

Commemorative plaque *on the office building near St. Giles in the Barbican.*

The German bombing raids on London that began in the summer of 1940 and continued throughout World War II are known as the Blitz. They destroyed much of historic London and many great cultural jewels. Buckingham Palace was bombed on September 13, 1940, and the King and Queen themselves shared the same terrible experience as the rest of the London population. "I'm glad we've been bombed," said the Queen. "Now I feel we can look the East End in the face." The eastern part of London had suffered particularly badly, as this part of the capital was near the docks on the Thames, which were considered a prime target for enemy bombing.

Much of the damage to wartime London has long since been repaired, but some areas of London were so widely devastated that they were beyond repair. In the City of London areas of new development, like the Barbican, sit on areas of massive bomb damage. Memorial plaques on buildings record some of these bombing raids. Underground stations once used as bomb shelters are still in everyday use today, and some of the older stations, like the Elephant & Castle, can evoke the feeling of what it must have been like to shelter here as bombs shook the ground above. Both the Imperial War Museum and the Britain at War Museum on the south side of the Thames contain simulations of what it was like during the Blitz, as well as collections of memorabilia from this period.

Wartime photographs show St. Paul's Cathedral in the heart of London swathed in smoke during the Blitz, and the fact that this magnificent building never suffered direct bomb damage was perceived as a minor miracle symbolizing London's defiance. The modern development directly to the north of the Cathedral was a bomb-damaged site.

PLAN OF BATTLE

The German air assault on Britain in the summer of 1940 was intended as the prelude to an invasion of the country called Operation Sea Lion. The intention was to destroy the R.A.F. and thus remove Britain's air defenses, allowing for a fleet to sail across the Channel and for German troops to execute a land invasion of southern England, resulting in the capture of London. The first targets for the German air force were R.A.F. bases, but when the *Luftwaffe* failed to beat British air defenses, it turned its attention to terror bombing campaigns over London and other major industrial cities in Britain.

- RAF Fighter Command group headquarters
- RAF Fighter base
- Luftwaffe Fighter base
- Luftwaffe Bomber base
- Blitzed cities

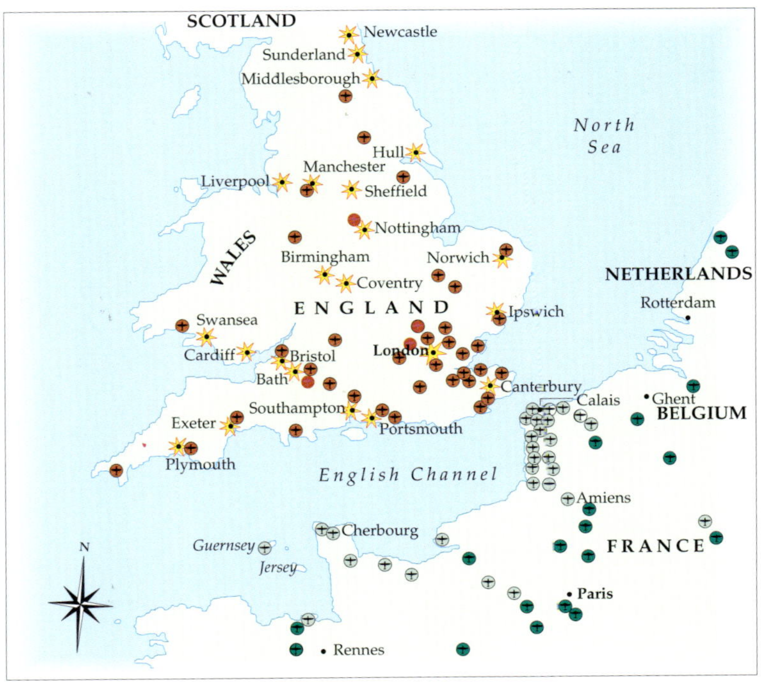

LONDON BLITZ

THE CITY OF LONDON TODAY is a bustling financial center, but in the summer of 1940, during the bombing raids of the Blitz, it became a terrifying inferno of explosions and uncontrollable fires. Buildings collapsed on rescuers, and victims were buried for days beneath rubble. The city has long recovered from this ordeal, but scars of its experiences then can be still be seen.

GETTING THERE

LOCATION: *Central London, U.K.*

VISITOR INFORMATION: *London Tourist Board, Glen House, Stag Place, Victoria, London SW1E 5LT*

TELEPHONE: *020 7932 2000*

DIRECTIONS: *Start your tour at Barbican Underground Station.*

TOUR DISTANCE: *8½ miles (14km).*

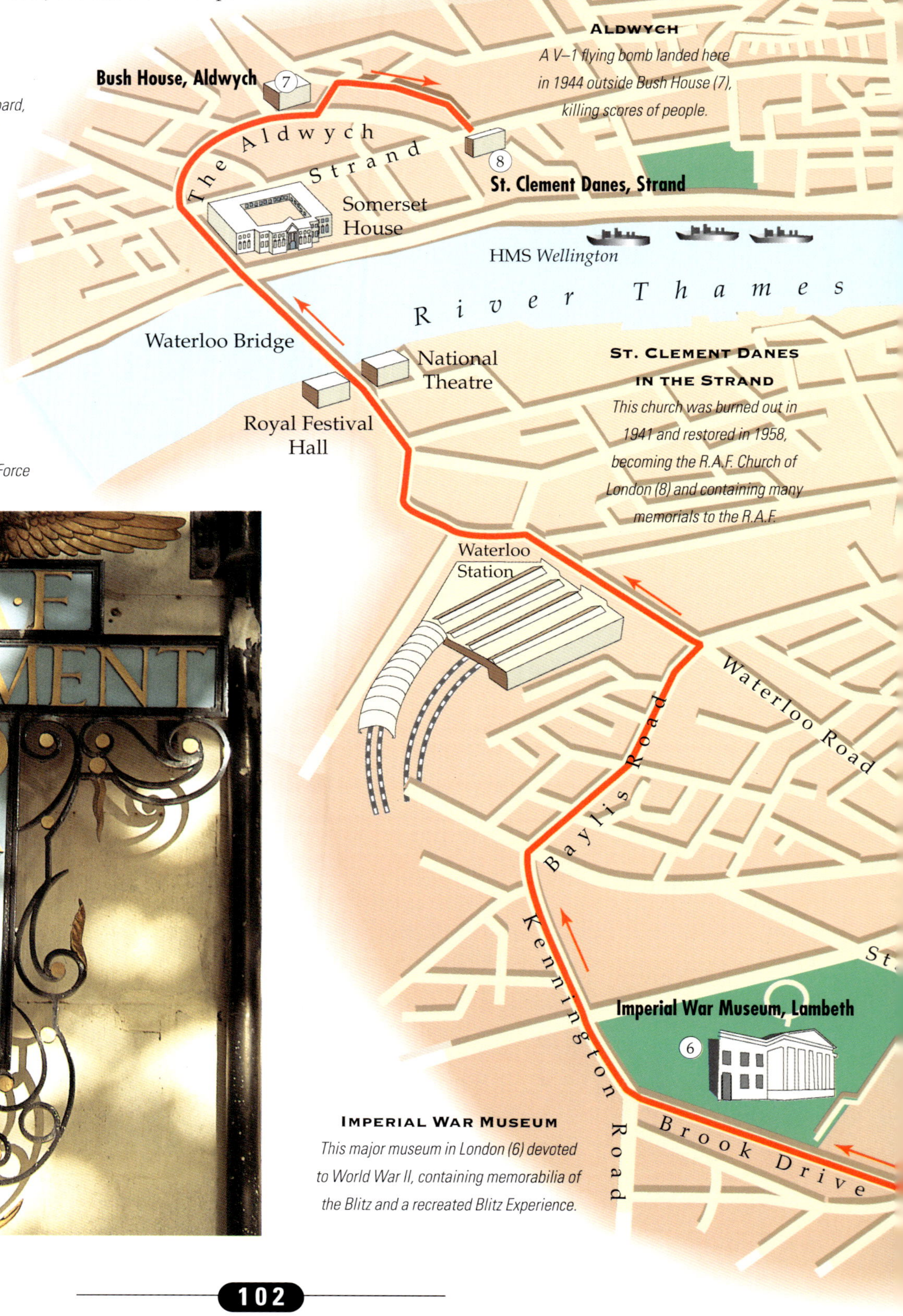

BELOW ***Memorials*** *to the Royal Air Force*

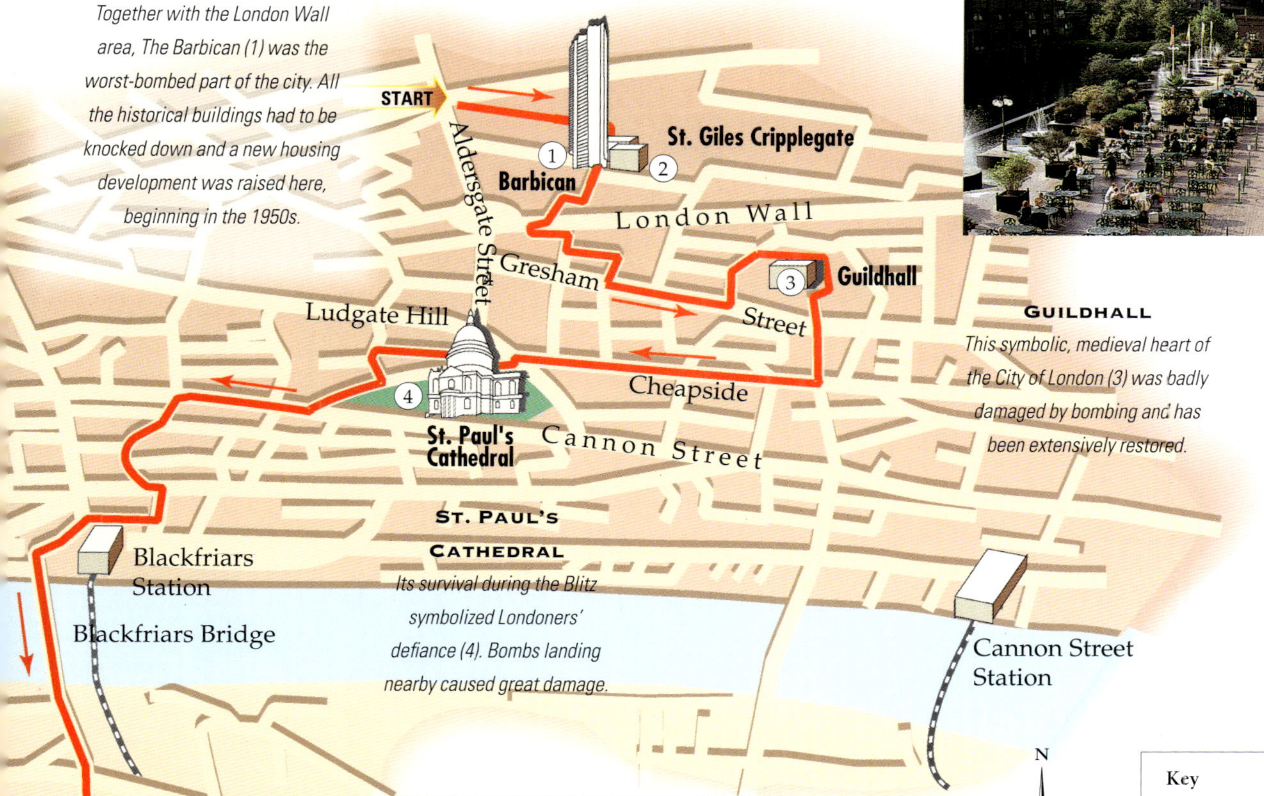
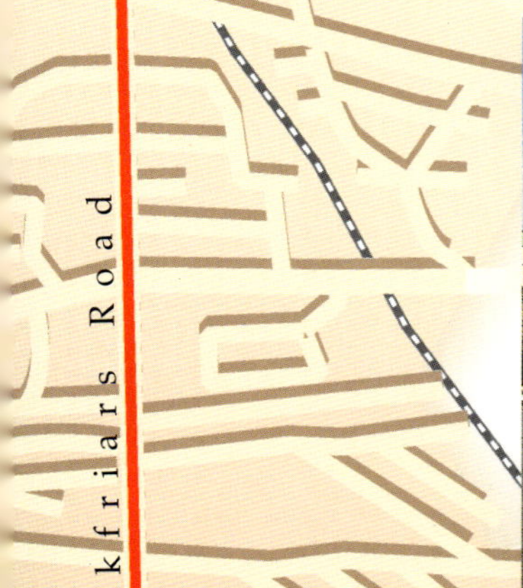
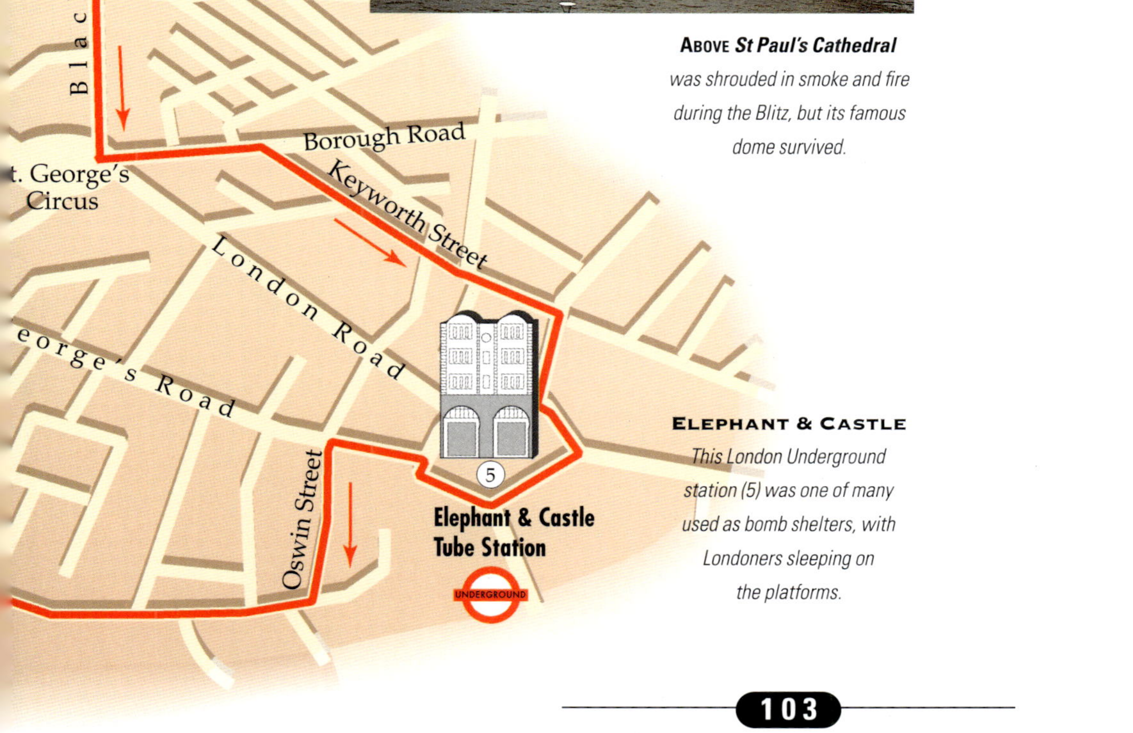

The Barbican

Together with the London Wall area, The Barbican (1) was the worst-bombed part of the city. All the historical buildings had to be knocked down and a new housing development was raised here, beginning in the 1950s.

Above *The Barbican* *was the worst bombed part of the city and is now completely rebuilt.*

Guildhall

This symbolic, medieval heart of the City of London (3) was badly damaged by bombing and has been extensively restored.

St. Paul's Cathedral

Its survival during the Blitz symbolized Londoners' defiance (4). Bombs landing nearby caused great damage.

Above *St Paul's Cathedral* *was shrouded in smoke and fire during the Blitz, but its famous dome survived.*

Below *Elephant and Castle* *underground where Londoners sheltered from bombing.*

Elephant & Castle

This London Underground station (5) was one of many used as bomb shelters, with Londoners sleeping on the platforms.

JOHN FROSTBRUG

BRIDGE TOO FAR

Above ***General Montgomery*** *masterminded Operation Market Garden, which sent Allied airborne troops to capture vital bridges across the Rhine. Portrait painted in 1942 by Captain Neville Lewis.*

Left ***Modern traffic crosses the bridge at Arnhem*** *that cost so many lives.*

The Allies had broken out of Normandy, and Paris was liberated, but in the late summer of 1944 the victorious Allied advance was running out of steam. The Americans wanted to advance on a broad front into Germany, but Field Marshal Bernard Montgomery wanted to end the war more quickly with a swift advance against the industrial center of Germany in the Ruhr. Rather than tackling the Siegfried line, he recommended an assault through the Netherlands around the northern flank of Germany's defensive line. The supreme Allied commander, General Dwight D. Eisenhower, was finally persuaded to back this venture, and it was called Operation Market Garden. It was to be the largest use of Allied airborne troops in World War II.

AIRBORNE ASSAULT

A crucial aspect of this operation was the seizure of key bridges into Germany. This involved dropping paratroopers behind the German lines and capturing the bridges before they could be destroyed. Two U.S. airborne divisions—the 101st and the 82nd—were aimed at bridges near Eindhoven, Grave, and Nijmegen in Holland, while the British First

BACKGROUND TO BATTLE

The aim behind Operation Market Garden was to end the war in Western Europe by Christmas 1944. The landing at Normandy and the hard fighting to break out of there and liberate France had demonstrated that the Germans would not give in easily, and the end of the war would be very costly in terms of Allied lives, a deeply unpopular sacrifice which would adversely affect public opinion in Britain and the United States. It was perhaps this reasoning that persuaded Eisenhower to allow Montgomery to press ahead with his airborne assault on bridges in the Netherlands.

If the operation succeeded, then the British Second Army could outflank the Siegfried Line and enter the North German plain. The industrial powerhouse of the Ruhr could then be captured and a more direct route opened to Berlin, allowing the Allies to reach it before the Russians and thus alter the balance of power at the beginning of the Cold War. It was a lot to play for, but had Montgomery overestimated the abilities of his paratroopers?

Background ***Aerial view of the ramp*** *of the bridge at Arnhem leading into the city center littered with wrecked vehicles of the Ninth SS Panzer Division destroyed by British paratroopers.*

Airborne Division was to capture the most northerly bridges at Arnhem. Maj. General Robert Urquhart was in command of the British force numbering some 10,000, but he had no experience of airborne assaults and made several crucial mistakes in the preparation of the attack on Arnhem. The R.A.F. could not deliver all his men in one drop and, concerned about antiaircraft guns, they dropped them eight miles west of the town, necessitating a long march to reach their objectives. Finally, he ignored intelligence that told him that the Dutch town was more heavily defended by Germans than they had initially expected.

Gliders brought many of the British soldiers into the countryside west of Arnhem on September 17. At first they were greeted by the jubilant Dutch, but their advance toward Arnhem was then checked by the fire of German snipers and they were forced to slow

Above ***British airborne troops*** *enter an Airspeed Horsa glider of the type that landed near Arnhem.*

CAUGHT IN THE BATTLE

Dutch civilians were happy to see British paratroopers arrive in Arnhem, but when the battle started they were forced to hide in their cellars and endure horrific scenes. Bertje Voskuil remembers sheltering in a cellar with British soldiers when the Germans burst in:

"I heard them fighting in the house above us—shots and screams; they made all sorts of noises when they were fighting, sometimes just like animals. Then the door burst open and the Germans came in. A tall British soldier jumped in front of me...There were two terrific explosions then—German grenades. The British soldier was hit in the back and fell forward over me. He was dead. Many of the people in the cellar were wounded. I was hit in both legs, and my hearing was affected—and still is...Then a German officer called out to me, 'Do you speak English?' I said I did, and he told me to translate quickly, to tell the English that they had fought gallantly and had behaved like gentlemen, but they must surrender now and hand over their weapons."

Quoted in ARNHEM 1944: THE AIRBORNE BATTLE *by Martin Middlebrook (Viking, 1994).*

British paratroopers, *exhausted and wounded, are taken prisoner by the Germans at Arnhem.*

down. When they reached the train bridge, it was blown up before their eyes. There remained the massive road bridge in the center of the town and Company A of the Second Parachute Battalion commanded by Lt. Col. John Frost raced toward it, only to be met by heavy fire from German machine guns.

Frost dug in and waited for reinforcements, but they were never to arrive, being halted by the 9th SS Panzer Division, which had stopped nearby to recuperate after heavy fighting in France. Further British paratroopers were killed as they floated down from their aircraft. Captain Harry Roberts of the Royal Engineering and Mechanical Corps was shot as he emerged from his glider: "As soon as we landed I jumped out, whilst the glider was still rolling, followed by driver Gould and Craftsman Tracy-Bower. There was a burst of fire from a Spandau which fatally wounded Gould and hit me in the spine...Although the bullet was fired from point-blank range, I was probably flexing in mid-air when it hit me, and it went through the rubber folds of the gas mask which we carried across the small of our backs." [Roberts survived the wound, but was paralyzed from the waist down and captured by the Germans.]

Frost now had to face heavy fighting with just 500 men. A bitter struggle erupted around the bridge as both sides attempted to occupy it. Using armored cars and half-tracks, the Germans eventually managed to force their way across the bridge, and Frost came under increasingly heavy fire from tanks.

Sapper George Needham, hidden in a school, recalled the shock of being fired at by a German tank: "Suddenly, there was a terrific explosion underneath this flight of stairs. It was the first time the building had been hit by such a big shell. There was a tank on the ramp [of the bridge] firing at point-blank range. We had been used to small arms fire and mortaring, but it was absolutely stunning when this huge explosion took place. There was dust everywhere, and it was several seconds before I realized what had happened. I didn't even know the tank was outside. It says a lot for the quality of Dutch building that the school didn't collapse."

ABOVE ***John Frost's Bridge****, named after the British commander of Paratroopers who fought for the original bridge in 1944.*

DESPERATE DEFENSE

Urquhart himself was trapped in the attic of a house for a crucial thirty-six hours by the presence of German tanks and only managed to reach the Hartenstein Hotel on September 19. By then, the British had lost the initiative and were strung out around Arnhem under heavy fire. Supplies meant for them were dropped into German hands, and communication was severely disrupted.

Urquhart decided to form a defensive perimeter around the Hartenstein Hotel, three miles west of the Arnhem Bridge, and ordered the rest of the paratroopers to withdraw there. Frost was isolated at the bridge under increasingly intense fire from Tiger tanks destroying the buildings that were hiding his troops. Reduced to some 150 fighters with ammunition running out, it was a desperate situation. A brigade of Polish paratroopers landed south of the river too late to affect the outcome of the battle, and became casualties themselves.

Denied sleep or proper food for four days, the paratroopers at the Hartenstein Hotel were beginning to weaken. Geoffrey Powell in C Company of the Parachute Battalion recalls the sense of desperation: "The discovery that there was no food made me aware once more of a stomach which was very empty indeed. As our party edged its way back to the others, first through the Hartenstein grounds, then the dash across the main road, followed by the cautious progress through the silent side streets, it was hard to keep my mind off that last and only meal, eaten over twenty-four hours before. During the day I had been too busy to remember my hunger, but the knowledge that there were no rations had reawakened a dormant appetite in a most perverse manner."

Montgomery had to accept the fact that his planned attack at Arnhem was a failure. He ordered Urquhart to withdraw across the river at night, but the Germans showed little mercy and bombarded the retreating men. By September 27 only 2,163 of the original 10,000 had made it to safety. Some 6,642 British and Polish soldiers were captured, wounded, or missing, and some 1,200 dead, all in a brave but fruitless battle. Elsewhere, the Americans had captured some of their objectives, but also met heavy German resistance. Arnhem had earned its name as a bridge too far.

ABOVE *Urquart's headquarters, Oosterbeek*, *now a museum to the battle for Arnhem.*

BELOW *Airborne Museum* *gate guardian in Oosterbeek.*

ARNHEM

German soldiers close *in on British paratroopers isolated near the bridge in Arnhem.*

THE PEOPLE OF ARNHEM will never forget the events of World War II. It's not just the famous bridge where British paratroopers fought a desperate last stand against SS armored divisions, but the whole town is a living memorial to Nazi occupation. Every family has a story to tell about how the Nazis looted houses and shops, stealing every stick of furniture.

The bridge at Arnhem is the focal point of any battlefield tour. Renamed the John Frost Bridge, after the commander of the British force surrounded there, it has been rebuilt since the war and has a memorial plaque in a concrete shelter on the west side. Along the road from the bridge to the city center is a circle in which a stone column is inscribed "17th September 1944". It is in this space that commemoration ceremonies are performed.

The most evocative memorials of the fierce days of fighting at Arnhem are located just outside the city in the quiet village of Oosterbeek. Here you will find the Commonwealth War Cemetery in which 1,757 British and Polish soldiers are buried. The main landings took place to the west of Oosterbeek in open fields more sparsely wooded than they are today.

Most of the Allied troops were trapped in Oosterbeek and the First Airborne's Divisional Headquarters was established at the Hartenstein Hotel. This is now an excellent museum commemorating the operation. It takes you through the German invasion of the Netherlands and the airborne landings. In the basement of the museum are superb recreations, including the first aid post, which was originally in the cellar of the hotel during the fighting.

The old church in the lower village at Oosterbeek has two memorials outside, one of which sums up the Dutch spirit of togetherness with the Allies, proclaiming: "Not one shall be forgotten."

PLAN OF BATTLE

Operation Market Garden employed paratroopers to strike the first blow, capturing vital bridges in the advance towards Germany. The ground forces led by XXX Corps would then follow through. At Arnhem, three separate parachute forces were dropped over three days, beginning on September 17. The Second Parachute Battalion under John Frost reached the main bridge at Arnhem but were cut off by strong SS Panzer forces. The rest of the British force formed a perimeter around the Hartenstein Hotel and fought a last stand there, some of the troops eventually retreating south across the river.

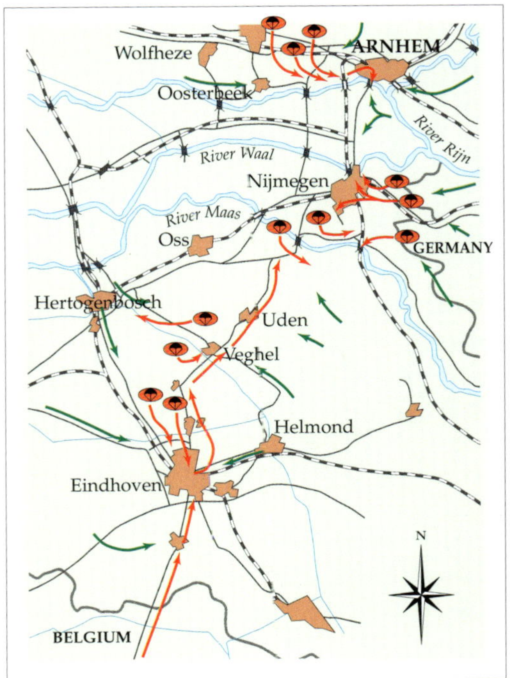

Allied advance
parachute and supply drop zone
German counterattack

0 10 km
0 10 miles

ARNHEM

THE DUTCH CITY OF ARNHEM suffered badly during World War II and its people have a special affection for the British who tried to liberate it. A warm welcome is assured for everyone visiting the sites and memorials to the events of September 1944.

EDE
British paratroopers landed here (7), many in gliders. Memorial opposite restaurant De Ginkel.

WAR CEMETERY
in Oosterbeek (6) containing British and Polish dead.

AIRBORNE MUSEUM
Situated in the Hartenstein Hotel (4) which, during the fighting was the Allied HQ and center of resistance.

BENEDENDORPSWEG CHURCH
Bitter fighting took place around the church (3), which now contains memorials.

GETTING THERE

LOCATION: *Arnhem, Netherlands.*

VISITOR INFORMATION: *Gelderland Board of Tourism, Staationsplein 45, P.O. Box 552, 6800 AN Arnhem.*

TELEPHONE: *026 4426767*

DIRECTIONS: *The John Frost bridge is on the south side of Arnhem. Oosterbeek is approximately 1 ¼ miles (2km) west of Arnhem. The no. 1 trolley bus goes from the railway station in Arnhem to the Airborne Museum in the Hartenstein Hotel, Oosterbeek.*

TOUR DISTANCE: *22 miles (35km).*

LEFT *Airborne Memorial at Ede,* *where many British paratroopers were shot and killed.*

Left *Airborne Monument*, *opposite the Hartenstein Hotel, remembers Paratroopers who sacrificed their lives at Arnhem.*

Right *British cemetery, Oosterbeek*, *also contains many Polish soldiers who fought with the British.*

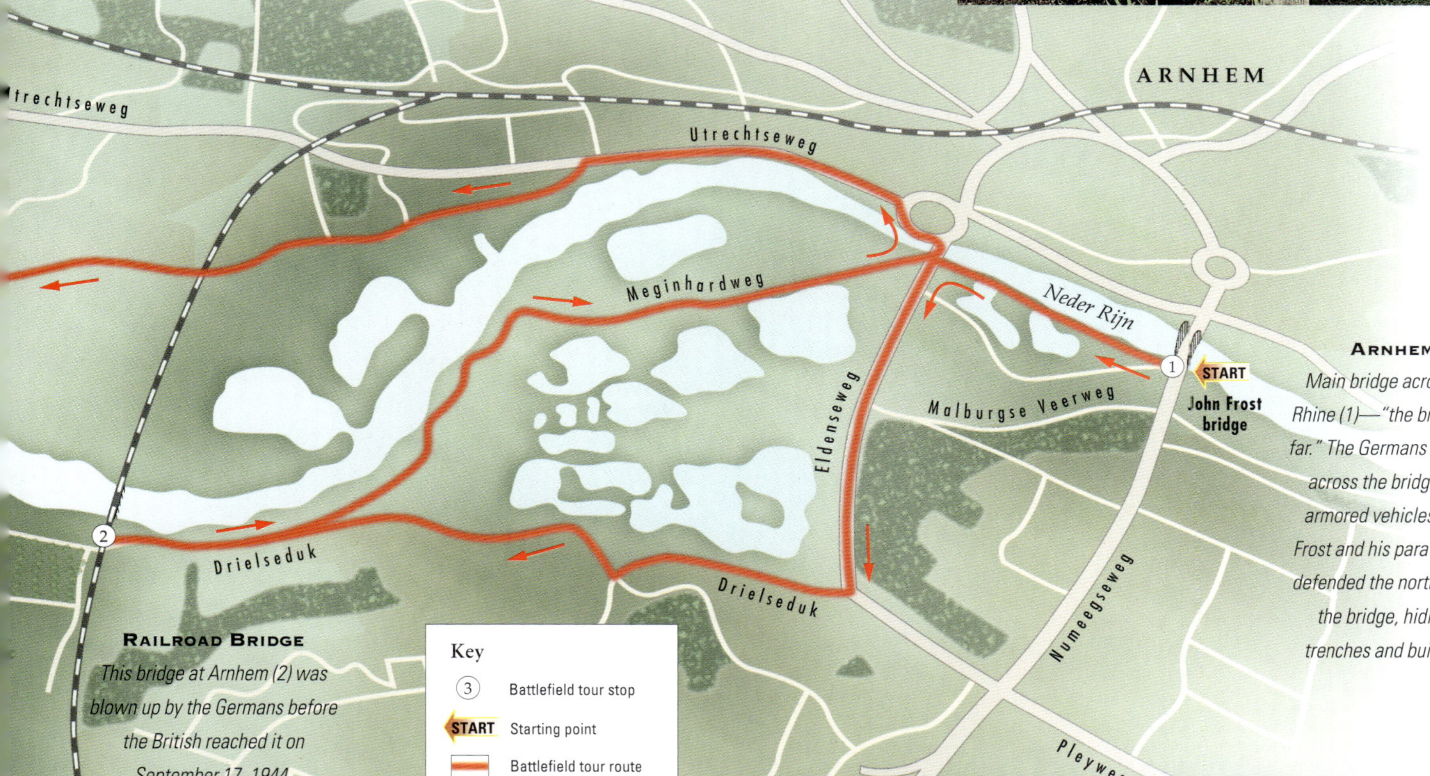

Arnhem

Main bridge across the Rhine (1)—"the bridge too far." The Germans attacked across the bridge with armored vehicles. John Frost and his paratroopers defended the north side of the bridge, hiding in trenches and buildings.

Railroad Bridge

This bridge at Arnhem (2) was blown up by the Germans before the British reached it on September 17, 1944.

Right *Railroad bridge, Oosterbeek*, *which was destroyed by the Germans in 1944 and rebuilt after the war.*

END OF THE THOUSAND YEAR REICH

ABOVE *Berlin postcard of 1933 showing the Reich Chancellery* *and a portrait of the newly elected Führer.*

LEFT *Russian troops raise the Red flag on top of the Reichstag building,* *the symbolic moment of victory. (Photograph by Yevgeni Khaldie.)*

ADOLF HITLER PROMISED the German people that his Nazi regime would last for a thousand years but, a mere six years after declaring war on the rest of Europe, he stood among the ruins of his capital awaiting the final crushing blows of the Soviet army in April 1945. And having suffered millions of casualties, both civilian and military to the German invaders, the Red Army was in no mood for mercy. It would be a savage final encounter.

FORMIDABLE TARGET

Since the turning point at Stalingrad in 1943, the Soviet army conducted a long and hard-won series of campaigns that pushed Hitler's war machine back into Germany. The German army had fought for every mile, knowing that a terrible retribution awaited them if they gave up to Soviet soldiers. When Marshal Georgi Zhukov, commander of the Red Army, visited Stalin, the Soviet leader, he could see that the dictator was exhausted and in a reflective mood, declaring: "What a terrible war. How many lives of our people it has carried away. There are probably very few families of us left who haven't lost someone near to them." Zhukov presented his plan of attack on Berlin to Stalin, who approved it on March 8, 1945.

BACKGROUND TO BATTLE

Since 1944, when German generals could see that they would lose the war, there had been a wish to reach a negotiated peace with the Allies and even an assassination plot was conceived to kill Hitler and end the war. Hitler's own last gamble had failed in the battle of the Bulge and he had grown ever more fatalistic, resigned to his own country and people being destroyed before the relentless advance of the Allied and Soviet armies.

Even as the Soviet army advanced towards Berlin in April 1945, Hitler was determined to keep on fighting and he prepared the capital with three massive defense lines. Antitank ditches and gun emplacements were hastily constructed along a 200-mile line from the Baltic to the Czech border. A vital aspect of this defense line was the Seelow Heights in front of Berlin. It was here that Russians would attack frontally.

It is possible that the Allies under Eisenhower could have reached Berlin before the Soviet army, but they feared that the desperate resistance promised by Hitler would create a sacrifice too high to justify to the soldiers' families back home. They also feared clashes with the Soviet army itself, for Stalin had grown increasingly distrustful of the West. As it was, the Russian capture of Berlin led to one of the first political hot spots in the Cold War that followed.

The plan was simple: Zhukov was to launch his attack from bridgeheads on the Oder and assault the city from the Seelow Heights. A separate flanking movement from the north was to curve round and attack the city from the west. General Ivan Konev, commander of the First Ukrainian Front, was to complete the encirclement of the city with a move from the south. There was strong rivalry between the two Soviet commanders about who would enter the city first.

It took two weeks to position the Soviet forces to attack Berlin. There were still some two million people left in the city and it was a formidable target to attack. There were a million German men ready to defend it, although many were very young and elderly volunteers. Hitler was still alive and deep in his bunker. Formidable barricades had been erected throughout the city and the German army still had over 1,500 tanks and 9,000 artillery pieces. But the Soviet army was expecting a stiff defense, having gathered over 14,000 guns, 3,000 tanks, and 1,500 rocket launchers. More than two million Soviet troops awaited the order to attack.

The attack came at dawn on April 14, 1945 with a massive artillery, aircraft, and rocket barrage. When the bombardment stopped, the Soviet soldiers found it difficult to cross the churned-up ground and, when they arrived at the first German defense line, they found it abandoned, meaning much of the assault had been wasted. Vehicles became bogged down in the mud and a dense cloud of dust and smoke obscured the view of the advance. Tanks could make little headway on the soft soil of the Seelow Heights and became vulnerable to German counterattacks with many losses among the Russian soldiers. Stalin was impatient and suggested Konev take the city from the south. Painfully slowly, Zhukov's men reached the outskirts of the city by April 20.

RIGHT Marshal Georgi Zhukov, commander of the Soviet forces that assaulted Berlin in April 1945. At first his plan to attack Berlin went too slowly for an impatient Stalin. Eventually his troops broke into the city, but at a high cost in casualties.

BELOW Russian soldiers raise the Red flag on top of the Brandenburg Gate, once the site of Hitler's victory parades. (Painting by Oleg Ponomarenko.)

RACE FOR THE CENTER

The Soviet Eighth Guards Army, led by General Vassily Chuikov, broke into the city and fought block by block towards the center. In the streets of Berlin, Germans used antitank rockets to great effect, and the Soviets had to improve their defenses by attaching sandbags or thin sheets of iron set at an angle on their tanks to deflect the rockets. Cornelius Ryan in *The Last Battle* effectively describes the brutal efficiency of the Russian advance: "Street barricades were

SUICIDE

As the Soviet army stormed into Berlin, many Germans feared terrible retribution. The Germans had treated the Soviet peoples mercilessly when they had invaded Russia, and now expected the worst. Vladimir Abyzov, a soldier in the Red Army, remembered storming an SS club in the center of the city:

> "Short of breath from running and excitement we rushed up the stairs to the second and third floors. Germans were firing at us from the top. But there were too many of us for them. The men running in front did not see those that fell below. In the billiard room candles were burning. Slumped over the green cloth of the table with yellow billiard balls on it was the dead body of a general, a pistol in his hand. He had shot himself."

From THE FINAL ASSAULT *by Vladimir Abyzov (Novosti, 1985).*

Russian propaganda poster *symbolizing the beginning of the Soviet counterattack against the Germans, which ended with the Red Army storming into Berlin.*

BACKGROUND *German prisoners stumble through the ruined streets of Berlin* *at the end of the battle for their capital.*

smashed like matchwood. Russian tanks, moving fast, blew up buildings rather than send soldiers in after snipers. The Red Army was wasting no time. Some obstacles, like tramcars and rock-filled wagons, were demolished by guns firing at point-blank range. Where more sturdy defenses were encountered, the Russians went around them. In Wilmersdorf and Schonenburg, Soviet troops encountering resistance entered houses on either side of the blocked streets and blasted their way from cellar to cellar with bazookas. Then they emerged behind the Germans and wiped them out."

By April 24, Chuikov's forces had crossed the Spree and Dahme rivers. Konev's troops were also battling their way into the center, much to Zhukov's consternation. They had an easier entry into the city. Under cover of artificial fog, they conducted an effective amphibious assault over the Neisse and then the Spree. On April 25, Konev directed his tanks toward the Reichstag and the center of Berlin. As his tanks opened fire, he was told he was firing on Soviet troops. The two Soviet commanders had met at the heart of Berlin. Konev had to call his men off, leaving it to General Chuikov and the Eighth Guards Army to take the center of the city.

The Soviet army now turned on the political center of the city, knowing that the Führer and leading Nazis were buried in their bunkers deep beneath the Reich Chancellery. Soviet troops were told that whoever raised the Red flag on the Reichstag building would be decorated as a Hero of the Soviet Union. Men of the 150th Rifle Division edged toward it through suicidal resistance. Under cover of thirty artillery guns, a small group of infantrymen burst into the Reichstag and, fighting hand to hand, secured the building floor by floor. After eight hours of fighting, Soviet troops reached the roof of the building and waved the Red flag in one of the most famous images of the war.

BELOW *With Germany reunited again* *after the end of the Cold War, the Reichstag building has once more become the seat of German government.*

On that same day, Hitler gathered his closest assistants and bade them farewell. He declared that the German people had let him down in this final test and that they deserved all that was coming to them. In a final grotesque ceremony he married his long-time mistress Eva Braun and together they entered his private rooms in the bunker. Eva Braun took poison, and Hitler shot himself in the head. Their bodies were then removed and burned in a shallow grave in the garden outside the bunker.

With Hitler dead, the German garrison now tried to negotiate an armistice with the Soviet commanders, who wanted nothing less than unconditional surrender. The Germans declared they would fight to the end and the Soviets unleashed every gun they could on the center of the city in a devastating firestorm. Only on the morning of May 2 did German defenders finally lay down their arms. The war was over. The citizens of Berlin had paid a heavy price for their final defiance with at least 100,000 civilians dead and an equal number of soldiers. The city was reduced to rubble and its people exposed to the brutal celebrations of the Soviet soldiers. They had endured enormous casualties in the last days of war, and vented their anger on Berliners, including mass rapes of German women.

BERLIN

Brandenburg Gate in the background
with the rubble of war strewn around it, including abandoned vehicles.

For almost fifty years, Berlin bore the scars of World War II. Germany was divided into four spheres of influence occupied by the Russians, Americans, British, and French. This arrangement was replicated in Berlin with the capital divided into four areas of Allied authority. The Russians held East Germany and East Berlin and in 1961, at the height of the Cold War, they hastily erected a wall that physically divided East from West Berlin. The Berlin Wall ran through the heart of the city and was only dismantled in 1989 with the collapse of the Soviet Union and the reunification of Germany.

The Berlin Wall in the center of the city ran close to the Reichstag, scene of the Soviet triumph. The Reichstag is now the seat of the unified German Parliament and has been recently restored. Nearby is the Brandenburg Gate through which Hitler had paraded his triumphant armies, and which had been a barricade during the Soviet assault on Berlin.

West along the road leading away from the Unter den Linden, called the Strasse des 17 Juni, is the Victory column or Siegessaule with its gilded, winged figure of Victory. The wide road itself was used for military parades and became an emergency airstrip during the assault on Berlin. The Victory column symbolizes both the beginning and end of German military aggression in the nineteenth and twentieth centuries. It was erected in 1872–3 to commemorate the rapid victories of the Prussian army over Denmark, Austria, and France, and the beginning of the German process of unification and foreign conquest which led to World War I and II. The gilded barrels of cannons captured in the war against France surround the column, and bronze friezes of military campaigns line its walls. But on close inspection of the marble base you can still see the scars left by shells and gunfire during the battle for Berlin in 1945.

Further west is the Berlin Olympic Stadium, scene of the infamous Nazi Olympics in 1936. Some of the Nazi emblems raised for this can still be seen there today, including a bell with the Nazi eagle on it.

PLAN OF BATTLE

The Soviet assault on Berlin consisted of a multi-pronged attack in which Zhukov's First Belorussian Front attacked from the east, north, and west and Konev's First Ukrainian Front attacked from the south. Both met in the center of the city, but Konev relented and allowed Zhukov's men to capture the Reichstag. Soviet and American troops linked up at Torgau on April 25, 1945.

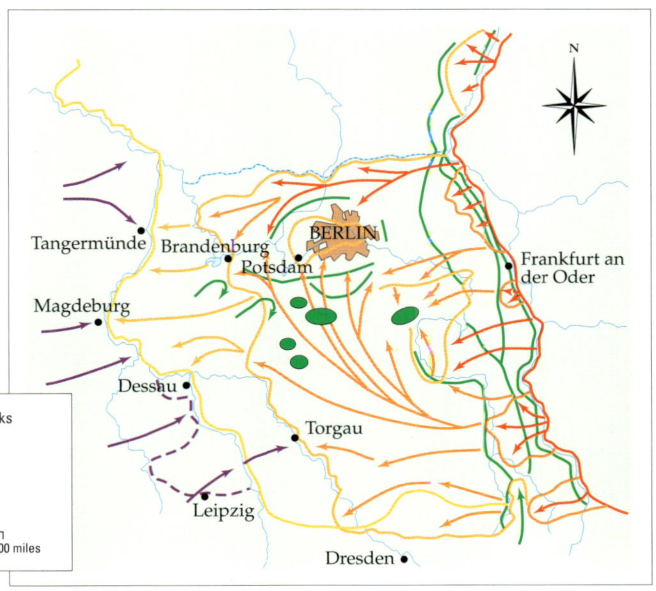

BERLIN

With the end of the Cold War and German reunification, Berlin is a busy building site with brilliant new skyscrapers rising in the center of the war-scarred capital. But you can still see some of the monuments that existed at the time of Hitler and the final battle for Berlin that ended World War II in Europe.

Olympic Stadium

Site of the notorious 1936 Berlin Olympics (6), in which Hitler hoped to impress the world with his Nazi regime. Several Nazi emblems from this time can still be seen there, including a bell from the bell tower, inscribed with a Nazi eagle.

GETTING THERE

Location: *Berlin, Germany.*

Visitor Information: *Tourist Information Office, Am Karlsbad No.11, 10785, Berlin.*

Telephone: *49 30 25 00 25*

Directions: *Begin your tour at the Reichstag, traveling by the U-bahn underground train system.*

Tour Distance: *7 miles (11km).*

Above ***Nazi sculpture of Aryan figures*** *raised outside the Berlin Olympic Stadium for the 1936 games, the most blatant Nazi emblems to survive the era.*

Below ***Berlin Olympic Stadium,*** *site of the notorious 1936 Olympics in which Hitler wished to demonstrate the success of his Nazi regime.*

ABOVE *New Reichstag building,* *the dome, designed by British architect Norman Foster, under contstruction.*

ABOVE *Original bell showing the Nazi eagle holding the Olympic rings.* *It hung in the 250-foot bell tower on the Maifeld overlooking the stadium, and rung out the opening of the games.*

SIEGESSAULE VICTORY COLUMN
This column (4) commemorates German victories in the late nineteenth century. Its marble base bears the marks of Soviet shells and gunfire from the final battle for Berlin. The wide road was used as an emergency airstrip.

BRANDENBURG GATE
Through this monument (2), Hitler's triumphant army marched in victory parades. In April 1945, it was reduced to a massive barricade. Between 1961 and 1989 it marked the point of division between West and East Berlin as the Berlin Wall ran nearby.

REICHSTAG
In 1933 the interior was gutted as Hitler finally grabbed political control of Germany (1). In 1945 it was pulverized as Soviet troops fought to capture it and then raise the Red flag on its roof. It has now been totally restored and is the seat of German democratic government once more.

SITE OF THE FLAK TOWER *near Berlin Zoo (5), a principal element of defense against the numerous Allied bombing raids that destroyed large parts of Berlin.*

AREA WHERE HITLER'S REICH CHANCELLERY *stood (3) and the bunker beneath it in which Hitler committed suicide.*

AFRICA AND ASIA

Battles in faraway lands have often brought out the very best in soldiers pitted against overwhelming odds.

At Rorke's Drift a legend of stubborn bravery was born that even the Zulus had to acknowledge. In Guam, U.S. Marines fought against the difficult terrain as much as its fanatical defenders. At Balaklava, mistakes were made, but no one could doubt the courage and devotion to duty of the Light Brigade as it charged into the jaws of death.

VALLEY OF DEATH

ABOVE *East end of North Valley* *looking up at Fediukine Heights. Over this highland came the first Russian attack.*

LEFT *Four survivors of the Seventeenth Lancers* *from the Charge of the Light Brigade. (Photo taken in 1856.)*

THE MOST FAMOUS CHARGE in the history of the British army took place during the battle of Balaklava. The Charge of the Light Brigade into the "valley of Death" is celebrated not for its triumph—it was a futile act—but for the way it demonstrated the bravery and duty of the British cavalry involved. Another incident in the battle demonstrated these British virtues more successfully—the Thin Red Line—making Balaklava the epitome of Victorian soldiering, both good and bad.

THIN RED LINE

If Russian sea power in the Black Sea was to be destroyed, then the port of Sevastopol on the Crimean peninsula had to be taken. British and French commanders acted together and put the port under siege in September 1854. The Russians came to the defense of their port slowly and were defeated at the battle of Alma. The Allies tightened their grip, establishing bases at the ports of Kamiesch and Balaklava. Receiving reinforcements, Prince Alexander Sergeievich Menshchikov, commander of the Russian forces in the Crimea, then decided to attack the British forces at Balaklava under the leadership of Lord Raglan, 1st Baron Fitzroy James Henry Somerset, and break the siege lines around Sevastopol.

On October 25, some 25,000 Russian infantry, thirty-four squadrons of cavalry, including Cossacks, and seventy-four pieces of artillery made a surprise attack on the British, based above the port of Balaklava. Raglan hadn't made enough fortified defenses for his troops and, when the Russians first appeared, they quickly took the outposts manned by the Allied Turkish soldiers. Russian cavalry now seized upon this impetus to

BACKGROUND TO BATTLE

The Crimean War was fought for global strategic reasons rather than because either Britain or France were directly threatened by Russia. Russia had long been making inroads into central Asia and the Balkans, and when they destroyed the Turkish fleet at Sinope, Britain feared a surge in Russian power in the Black Sea that could threaten her control of the Mediterranean. British and French fleets had arrived at Constantinople in 1853 to encourage the Turks, but with the imminent collapse of Turkish forces likely, both powers concluded a military alliance and declared war on Russia in the spring of 1854.

A Franco-British expeditionary force arrived in Varna to assist the Turks in repelling a Russian invasion of Bulgaria. Austria now threatened to join the alliance and Russia was compelled to retreat from Bulgaria. The British and French decided to take the war to Russia and invade the Crimea; their principal objective being the capture of the main Russian port of Sevastopol.

As the British and French forces awaited action against the Russians at Varna, they were devastated by disease and suffered acute shortages of food and poor shelter. The situation was desperate for allied soldiers in the Crimea.

drive home an attack on Colonel Sir Colin Campbell and his 93rd Highlanders, a mere 550 men drawn up in two lines to face 3,500 lancers, dragoons, and hussars.

William Russell, correspondent of the *London Times*, described what happened next: "The silence was oppressive; between the cannon bursts one could hear the champing of bits and the clink of sabres in the valley below. The Russians on their left drew breath for a moment, and then in one grand line charged in towards Balaklava. The ground flew beneath their horses' feet; gathering speed at every stride, they dashed on towards that thin red streak tipped with a line of steel. The Turks fired a volley at eight hundred yards and ran. As the Russians came within six hundred yards, down went that line of steel in front and out rang a rolling volley of Minie musketry [muzzle-loading rifles that fired conical bullets named after their inventor, French army officer, Captain Claude Etienne Minié]. The distance was too great; the Russians were not checked, but still swept onwards through the smoke, with the whole force of horse and man, here and there knocked over by the shot of our batteries above. With breathless suspense every one awaited the bursting of the wave upon the line of Gaelic rock; but ere they came within two hundred and fifty yards, another deadly volley flashed from the levelled rifles and carried terror among the Russians. They wheeled about, opened files right and left and fled faster than they came." This famous example of British courage was later immortalized in a painting by Robert Gibb in 1881 called *The Thin Red Line*.

"Their's Not to Reason Why"

A second Russian cavalry attack broke over the Causeway Heights and was met by the British Heavy Brigade, under Brigadier Sir James Scarlett. Once more, the British fought superior numbers, some 800 of them against 3,000 Russian horsemen, and put them to flight. This victory should have been followed through, but Brigadier General James T. Brudenell, 7th Earl of Cardigan, commander of the Light Brigade, watched the Russian retreat without making a move.

Frustrated, Lord Raglan urged Major General George Bingham, 3rd Earl of Lucan, overall commander of the British cavalry, to attack the land vacated by the Russians; but without infantry to support him, Lord Lucan declined to follow the order. This respite allowed the Russians time to pull up the artillery they had captured from the outlying redoubts. Raglan now sent Captain Louis Nolan with a written message to Lucan telling him to "advance rapidly to the front" and "prevent the enemy carrying away the guns."

Lucan could not see the guns that Raglan was referring to and assumed he meant a line of Russian artillery further away down the valley.

Above *Cornet John Wilkin of the Eleventh Hussars,* *one of the survivors of the Charge of the Light Brigade. (Photo by Roger Fenton in the camp at Balaklava.)*

Below *Port of Balaklava as it is today.* *During the Crimean War, it was packed with British sailing ships, but they failed to bring enough supplies for the British soldiers who suffered badly from disease and cold in their tents around the port.*

HEAVY BRIGADE IN ACTION

Richard Temple Godman was a young officer in the Fifth Dragoon Guards during the battle of Balaklava and, in a letter home to his father, describes taking part in the charge of the Heavy Brigade:

"The enemy seemed quite astonished [by the British attack] and drew into a walk and then a halt; as soon as they met, all I saw was swords in the air in every direction, the pistols going off, and everyone hacking away right and left. In a moment the Greys [Royal Scots Greys, a British cavalry unit] were surrounded and hemmed completely in; there they were fighting back to back in the middle, the great bearskin caps high above the enemy. This was the work of a moment; as soon as we saw it, the Fifth advanced and in they charged, yelling and shouting as hard as they could; the row was tremendous, and for about five minutes neither would give way, and their column was so deep we could not cut through it. At length they [the Russians] turned and well they might, and the whole ran as hard as they could pelt back up the hill, our men after them all broken up, and cutting them down right and left. We pursued about 300 yards, and then called off with much difficulty, the gunners then opened on them, and gave them a fine peppering."

Quoted from THE FIELDS OF WAR, *edited by Philip Warner (John Murray, 1977).*

The more successful, *but less well known of the British cavalry actions at Balaklava: the British Heavy Brigade take on superior numbers of Russian cavalry end force them back.*

Lucan thought this was madness and argued the point with Nolan, but Nolan insisted that Lucan attack, pointing into the distance. Reluctantly, Lucan ordered Cardigan to set the Light Brigade in motion and 673 cavalry of the 13th Light Dragoons, 17th Lancers, 4th, 8th, and 11th Hussars, started off at a trot. Realizing the mistake, Nolan dashed out in front of the cavalry, pointing to where they should attack but an enemy shot killed him and the cavalry thundered past him toward the line of Russian artillery.

"They advanced in two lines," wrote Russell, "quickening their pace as they closed towards the enemy. A more fearful spectacle was never witnessed than by those who, without the power to aid, beheld their heroic countrymen rushing to the arms of death. At the distance of 1,200 yards the whole line of the enemy belched forth, from thirty iron mouths, a flood of smoke and flame, through which hissed the deadly balls...we could see their sabres flashing as they rode up to the guns and dashed between them, cutting down the gunners as they stood."

It was a bold and courageous assault and lasted only twenty minutes, but one-third of the British cavalry were either killed or wounded. Both Lord Cardigan and Lucan were wounded. Confronted by a mass of Russian cavalry at the end of the valley, the British Light Brigade had no choice but to return to their lines. "It is magnificent," exclaimed French General Pierre Bosquet, witnessing the charge, "but it is not war." Sadly, with this one act, the British had lost the momentum of victory that the two earlier clashes had established. The Russians failed to move the British from Balaklava, but they had retained possession of the Vorontosov Ridge overlooking the road to Sevastopol.

The calamity of the Charge of the Light Brigade might well have remained a minor example of British military error had not the celebrated poet Alfred Tennyson written a poem about it. Inspired by Russell's description in *The Times*, he wrote an epic poem, which became popular among the soldiers in the Crimea and was later recited by generations of school children. "Their's not to make reply/ Their's not to reason why/ Their's but to do and die," declared Tennyson's poem, "Into the valley of Death/ Rode the six hundred."

BELOW *Aerial view of the Crimea* *published during the war in 1855 in the Illustrated Times.*

BALAKLAVA

THE MOST FAMOUS INCIDENT of the battle of Balaklava—the Charge of the Light Brigade—may well have occurred because of the geography of the battlefield. When Lord Lucan received Raglan's orders to "prevent the enemy carrying away the guns," Raglan was referring to the Russians on the Causeway Heights, but because Lucan and his Light Brigade were positioned on lower ground in the North Valley, he could not see these Russians and only saw the Russian artillery at the other end of the valley. It was on this mistake that the fatal charge began.

Visitors to the Crimean battlefield today can see it largely as it would have been at the time and make their own judgments on what could or could not have been viewed. The North Valley remains largely untouched farmland. The Causeway Heights are far gentler and lower than you might expect, but military historian Patrick Mercer still thinks there was a problem with observation: "I contend that under Nolan's impatient and ill-explained directions, the Brigade would have been put into motion easterly so that its commanders could get a better view of the ground and attempt to distinguish which guns it was that Raglan wanted to save. Under fire from almost the moment they started, however, and then suddenly assailed by guns to their front as the valley began to slow down, I suspect that the sheer impetus of the attack would have made it virtually impossible to divert, even up the comparatively gentle slopes of the Causeway Heights."

Raglan was situated on the higher Sapoune Ridge, which dominates the valley from the west, and could clearly see everything. The South Valley, in which the Heavy Brigade heroically repulsed the Russian cavalry, is more built up and it is less easy to trace British movements. At the point where the Heavy Brigade rose up on to the Causeway Heights, there is a simple, badly damaged, white stone monument, one of the few monuments in the Crimea raised by the British. For the Ukrainians who live here, there is little interest in the war, which they term the "First Defense of Sevastopol," the more visible remnants of battle belonging to the bitter fighting that took place during World War II against the Germans.

PLAN OF BATTLE

The battle of Balaklava began with a Russian advance over the river T'Chernaya and the Fediukine Heights, routing Turkish defenders. Pressing on into the South Valley, a massive formation of Russian cavalry captured redoubts on the Causeway Heights, but were then met by the British Heavy Brigade and Sir Colin Campbell's Thin Red Line. The Russian cavalry were thrown back over the Causeway Heights and retreated behind a line of artillery at the east end of the North Valley. Told to prevent the Russians removing captured artillery from the redoubts on Causeway Heights, the Light Brigade, on a misinterpreted order, charged along the North Valley at the main Russian artillery position, suffering terrible casualties. The Russians retained the Causeway Heights and control of the road to Sevastopol.

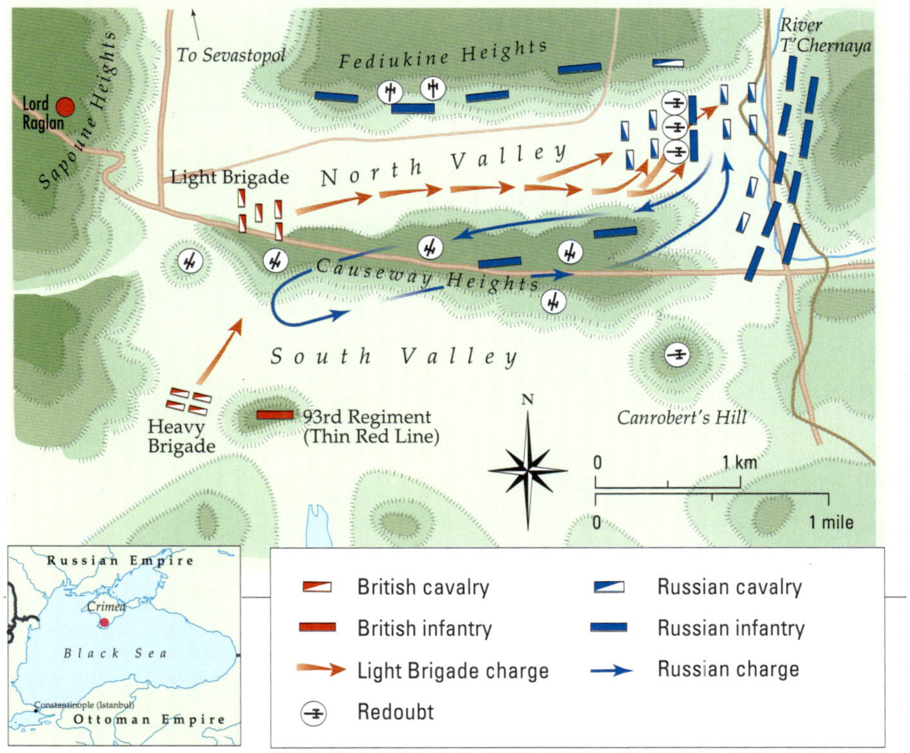

BALAKLAVA

THE BATTLEFIELDS OF THE CRIMEAN WAR are now part of the independent state of the Ukraine and it is best to visit them as part of an organized tour group. Once there, the visitor is rewarded by seeing a virtually unaltered valley in which the Light Brigade charged into legend.

NORTH VALLEY, WEST END
Light Brigade formed here (4). Lucan mistakenly ordered the Light Brigade along the North Valley toward the Russian artillery at the other end.

SOUTH VALLEY
The Heavy Brigade and the Ninety-third Highlanders—the Thin Red Line—both repulsed massive Russian cavalry assaults here (2), throwing them back over the Causeway Heights

GETTING THERE

LOCATION: *Crimea, Ukraine.*

VISITOR INFORMATION: *Tourist Office, 40b Franko Street, Kiev 01030, Ukraine.*

TELEPHONE: *044 238 6020*

DIRECTIONS: *International flight to Kiev, then internal flight to Sevastopol. Organized battlefield tour recommended.*

TOUR DISTANCE: *10 miles (16km).*

ABOVE *South Valley seen from the Causeway Heights.* *In the distance is the port of Balaklava. It was on this land that the Heavy Brigade and the 93rd Highlanders bravely fought off a massive Russian cavalry attack.*

PORT OF BALAKLAVA
The British fleet was anchored here (1) during the war, with Cardigan retiring after the Charge of the Light Brigade to his luxury yacht where he bathed and drank champagne to raise his spirits. Ordinary British soldiers were not so well looked after and suffered in tents around the port.

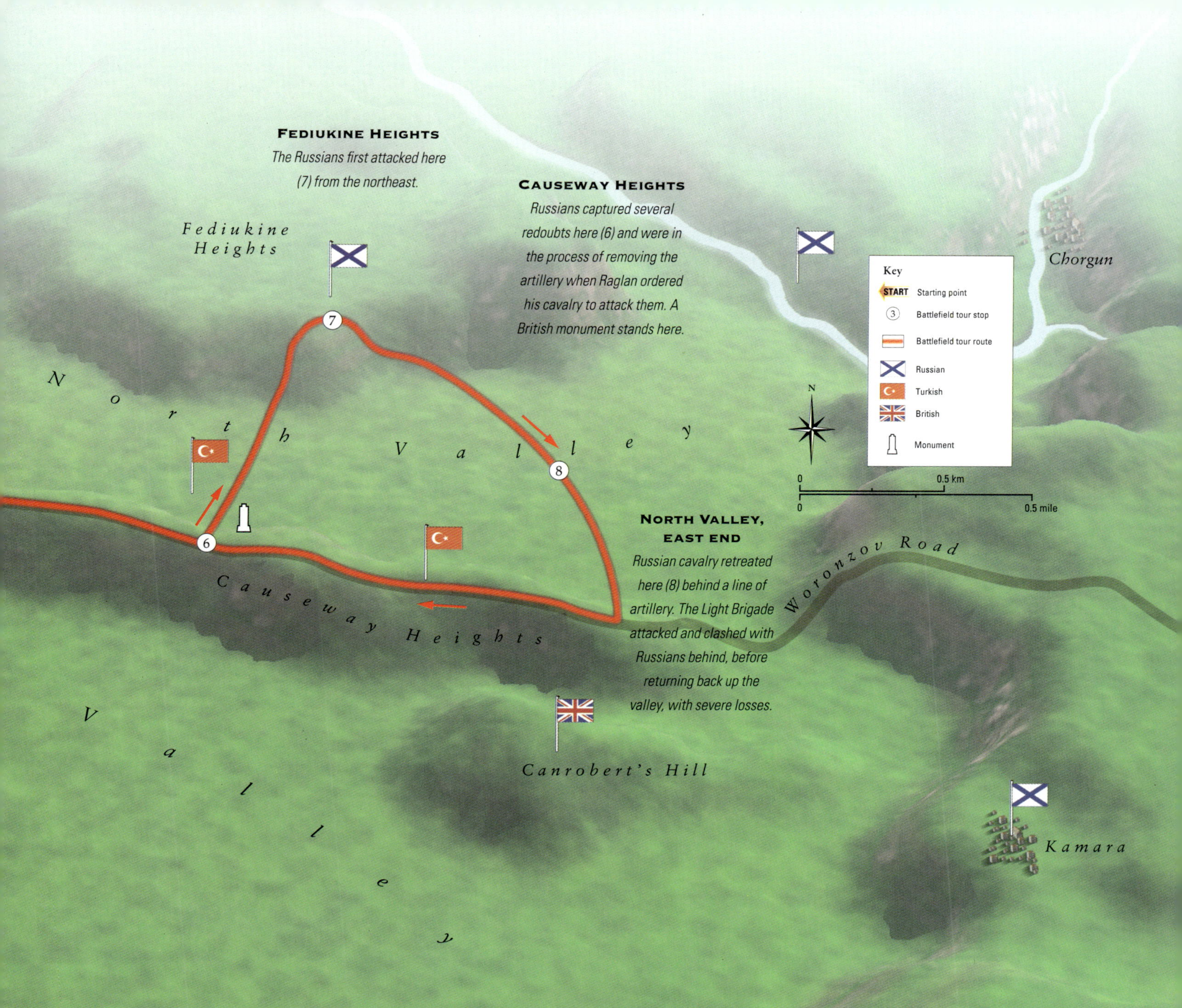

Below ***Russian artillery position,*** *looking west along the North Valley, with the Causeway Heights to the left. Over this land charged the Light Brigade "into the jaws of Death."*

Below ***Valley of Death.*** *In the distance is Raglan's position on the Sapoune Ridge, marked by a slight V in the trees on the horizon to the right.*

AGAINST ALL ODDS

ABOVE ***Private Alfred Henry Hook*** *bravely defended the hospital at Rorke's Drift until forced to retreat, helping patients escape from the burning building and winning a Victoria Cross for his actions.*

LEFT ***Scene from the classic film*** **Zulu** *recreating the stand at Rorke's Drift (Paramount Pictures, 1963). Zulu warriors attack the British behind their wall of mealie bags and biscuit crates.*

THE DEFENSE OF RORKE'S DRIFT is one of the great feats of arms of the British Army and was immortalized in the classic film *Zulu*. But certainly the handful of defenders of this little outpost can hardly have expected anything like the onslaught that was to descend upon them. At the beginning of the war against the Zulus in 1879, the British commander, Lieutenant General Frederic Augustus Thesiger Lord Chelmsford, had crossed the frontier into Zululand and been grateful to find the little settlement nearby. He left less than a hundred soldiers there to transform it into a supply depot and hospital. Days later, one of Chelmsford's columns was overwhelmed by a massive Zulu attack and 1,329 soldiers were slaughtered at Isandlwana. The Zulus had tasted blood, but their reserve component, the uNdi Corps under Prince Dabulamanzi kaMpande, had not taken part in the victory. Seeking another opportunity to strike at the "red soldiers," the uNdi Corps moved toward the little outpost at Rorke's Drift.

FORTY TO ONE

Before the soldiers came, Rorke's Drift was occupied by a Swedish missionary who lived in one of the buildings and used the other as a church. The soldiers turned the chapel into a store, loaded with mealie

BACKGROUND TO BATTLE

As the British Empire grew in southern Africa, so it inherited the problems of its white settlers. For years the Boers had clashed with the Zulus, and as the British extended their control over Boer land so they had to deal with Cetewayo kaMpande, King of the Zulus. In southern Africa, there was no concept of land ownership among the native tribes—it could neither be bought nor sold, but belonged to whoever farmed it. Thus, when the Boers farmed land, it became theirs.

Cetewayo was determined not to give up his people's farming rights to their land but, on December 11, Britain delivered an ultimatum to him, demanding to establish a protectorate over Zululand. Cetewayo ignored the ultimatum and, on January 11, Lord Chelmsford led an army of 5,000 British and 8,000 native troops into Zululand. Cetewayo commanded some 40,000 warriors and at Isandlwana on January 22, Chelmsford's central column was wiped out. Later that day, Dabulamanzi's Zulus moved from Isandlwana to Rorke's Drift on the way toward Natal. They expected an easy victory. Cetewayo, however, did not want his warriors threatening Natal, as he believed it would strengthen British resolve to fight. When he learned of Dabulamanzi's attack on Rorke's Drift, Cetewayo dispatched an order to recall the uNdi Corps.

(corn) bags and biscuit boxes. The house was transformed into a hospital, where a surgeon and three men of the Army Hospital Corps looked after thirty-five sick men. The post was guarded by eighty men of B Company, 2/24th under the command of Major Spalding. On the morning of January 22, 1879, Spalding had to ride off in search of reinforcements, leaving Lieutenant John Chard of the Royal Engineers in charge. "I see you are senior," he said to Chard, "so you will be in charge, although, of course, nothing will happen and I shall be back again this evening early."

Throughout the same day, some miles away, Zulu warriors overwhelmed an entire British column. One group of Zulus, however, had not been directly involved in the battle and were hungry for a victory of their own. The uNdi Corps was comprised of young warriors in their early thirties who were unmarried—the iNdluyengewe—and seasoned veterans in their forties. Commanded by Prince Dabulamanzi

BELOW *British soldiers hold their improvised* *perimeter wall at Rorke's Drift while the hospital burns behind them. (Painting by Alphonse de Neuville.)*

Right *Ruins of the storehouse* *at Rorke's Drift, photographed a few months after the battle when the outpost had been further strengthened with a stone wall.*

kaMpande—the ambitious brother of the Zulu king, Cetewayo—they surged across the Mzinyathi river toward Rorke's Drift. Just ahead of them were two Natal riders who burst into Rorke's Drift with news of the disaster.

Chard hastily ordered his soldiers to create a fortification out of the stores of mealie sacks and biscuit boxes. These barricades were impressive, rising above the height of a man with firing platforms constructed behind them. A few more Natal horsemen rode into the outposts and joined the defenders, but others simply rode past in a panic, encouraging the others to leave. There were now less than 150 defenders left against 4,000 approaching Zulus, odds of nearly forty to one.

STUBBORN DEFENSE

It was 4:30 in the afternoon when the Zulu wave crashed upon Rorke's Drift. "uSuthu!

RIFLES AND BAYONETS

Private Alfred Henry Hook was one of the defenders of Rorke's Drift who won a Victoria Cross for his bravery. In an interview with the *Royal Magazine*, he described the problems the British soldiers had with their weapons:

"I need hardly say that we were using Martinis, and fine rifles they were, too. But we did so much firing that they became hot, and the brass of the cartridges softened, the result being that the barrels got very foul and the cartridge-chamber jammed. My own rifle was jammed several times, and I had to work away with the ramrod till I cleared it. We used the old three-sided bayonet, and the long, thin blade that we called the 'lung' bayonet. They were fine weapons, too; but some were very poor in quality, and either twisted or bent badly. Several were like that at the end of the fight; but some terrible thrusts were given, and I saw dead Zulus who had been pinned to the ground by the bayonets going through them."

Quoted in MARCHING TO THE DRUMS *by Ian Knight (Greenhill Books, 1999).*

Breech of Martini-Henry *rifle. Although praised by the soldiers who used it at Rorke's Drift, its superior firepower was let down by constant overheating and jamming.*

ABOVE *This building,* *raised on the foundations of the old hospital at Rorke's Drift, closely resembles the original, except for the thatched roof which was set on fire. Many of the most determined Zulu attacks took place across this ground.*

uSuthu!" ("Kill! Kill!") chanted the black warriors as they ran toward the rear of the outpost. The British soldiers held their fire until they were within yards and then let loose a fierce volley, sending many of the Zulus somersaulting back into their ranks. But still the Zulus came on, trampling over their dead and wounded. Some Zulus occupied the Oskarberg terraces above the outpost and fired down at the soldiers, wounding many and killing a few. But as the firefight progressed, the antiquated muzzle-loading rifles of the Zulus were outperformed by the British Martini-Henry rifles.

As wave after wave of Zulu warriors rushed the defenses, the dead bodies piled in front of the barricades and other Zulus used them as a ramp to get closer to the British. After several hours of fighting, Chard was forced to withdraw his men behind the inner barricade, leaving the hospital open to direct attack, with only a handful of fit men inside to protect the sick and wounded. The Zulus began to break down the hospital door. While his mates retreated to another room, taking the wounded with them, Private Joe Williams stood at the door and kept the Zulus at bay with his bayonet. After killing a dozen warriors, Williams was grabbed and dragged outside, where he was spread-eagled on the ground and stabbed to death with assegais.

The Zulus pressed on to the next door in the hospital. As they broke through, they were met by Private Alfred Hook who shot half a dozen of the enemy. A spear pierced his helmet and injured his head, but Hook fought on like a demon, shooting and lunging with his bayonet as his comrades retreated to yet another room, dragging the wounded with them. By now, the Zulus had set fire to the hospital roof, but the defenders had managed to reach the last room by making holes in the partition walls, and lifted the wounded out of the building. Under heavy fire, they covered the last thirty yards to the inner barricades where Chard and his men were still holding out.

As night fell, the attacks continued relentlessly. Fire illuminated some of the attacks, but other assaults loomed terrifyingly out of the darkness. Exhausted, but well supplied with ammunition, the redcoats kept up their withering fire and when the Zulus clambered to the tops of the barricades, the British plunged their bayonets into them. It was a bitter and ferociously bloody struggle, which the British would not give up.

An hour before dawn, the Zulu attacks faltered and quiet descended on the outpost. When daylight came, it revealed a scene of devastation with piles of bodies spread about Rorke's Drift. Later, Lord Chelmsford appeared with a column of British soldiers. Fearing the worst, he was relieved to hear a cheer rise from behind the barricades. The Zulus drifted away and would not return. At least 400 Zulus had been killed. Chard had lost seventeen men dead and most were wounded. Among the British were many heroes, and some eleven Victoria Crosses were awarded to the stubborn defenders, including Chard and Hook.

RORKE'S DRIFT

ABOVE *Cetewayo, King of the Zulus,* *was furious with his warriors for suffering so many casualties at Rorke's Drift without achieving anything.*

Visiting Rorke's Drift today, it is clear why Lord Chelmsford decided to site his supply post there. It is the best crossing point for miles across the Mzinyathi River, or Water of the Buffaloes as it is known in Zulu. Upstream, the river that marked the old border of Zululand runs through rolling hills, while downstream from the Drift it enters a narrow gorge. This was the easiest place for Chelmsford to enter Zululand.

A mission station in 1879, the buildings at Rorke's Drift today are still a working mission. Other buildings have grown around it, but at the time of the battle there were only two buildings there: the hospital and the storehouse. Neither of the original buildings survived the battle, the hospital being burned down and the storehouse demolished when the missionaries returned. New buildings have been built on the foundations of the old structures. The house on the site of the hospital looks remarkably like the original building and now contains an excellent battlefield museum. The British cemetery for the soldiers who died in the battle stands next to these buildings. Markers have been placed to indicate the approximate site of Zulu graves, but recent excavations have revealed no bodies. The Oskarberg remains, the terrace behind the building that the Zulus first occupied and fired down from. It was this Zulu fire, managing to penetrate inside the British defenses, that compelled Chard to retreat to his final redoubt in front of the storehouse, thus screening himself from the Zulu snipers. The overall fragility of the position says much for the bravery of its defenders who would not give it up to an overwhelming Zulu force.

PLAN OF BATTLE

At Rorke's Drift, Lieutenant Chard created a surprisingly effective fortified outpost by utilizing the mealie bags, biscuit crates, and wagons that had been left there as supplies for Chelmsford's army. Just over a hundred men defended the improvised perimeter against 4,000 Zulus. The initial onslaught came from the rear of the outpost, and by nightfall the Zulus had it completely surrounded. During the evening, British soldiers retreated from the hospital to an inner barricade near the storeroom.

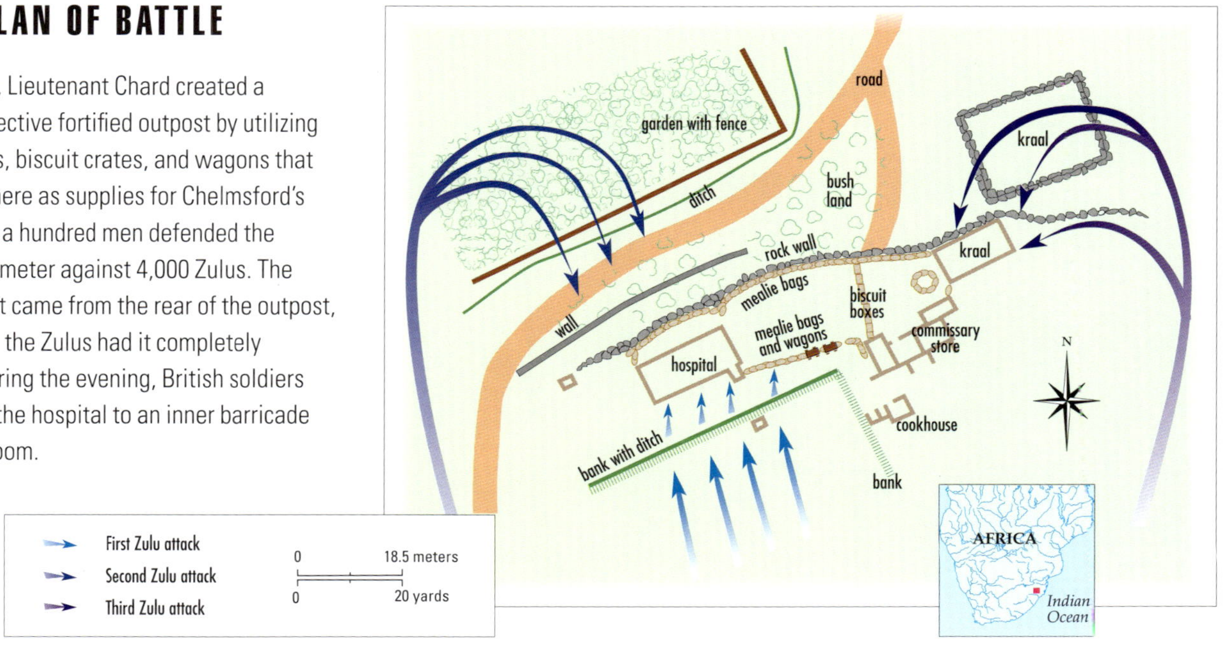

RORKE'S DRIFT

THE REMOTENESS OF RORKE'S DRIFT, some 30 miles (50 kilometers) from the nearest town, Dundee, makes it a difficult place to visit as an independent traveler, and an organized tour is strongly recommended to get the most from the battlefield.

GETTING THERE

LOCATION: *KwaZulu-Natal, Republic of South Africa.*

VISITOR INFORMATION: *KwaZulu-Natal Tourism Authority, P.O. Box 2516, Durban, 4000, South Africa.*

TELEPHONE: *031 304 7144*

DIRECTIONS: *By car, drive north from Durban to Dundee, then follow road just over 30 miles northeast to Buffalo river.*

TOUR DISTANCE: *0.3 miles (0.5km).*

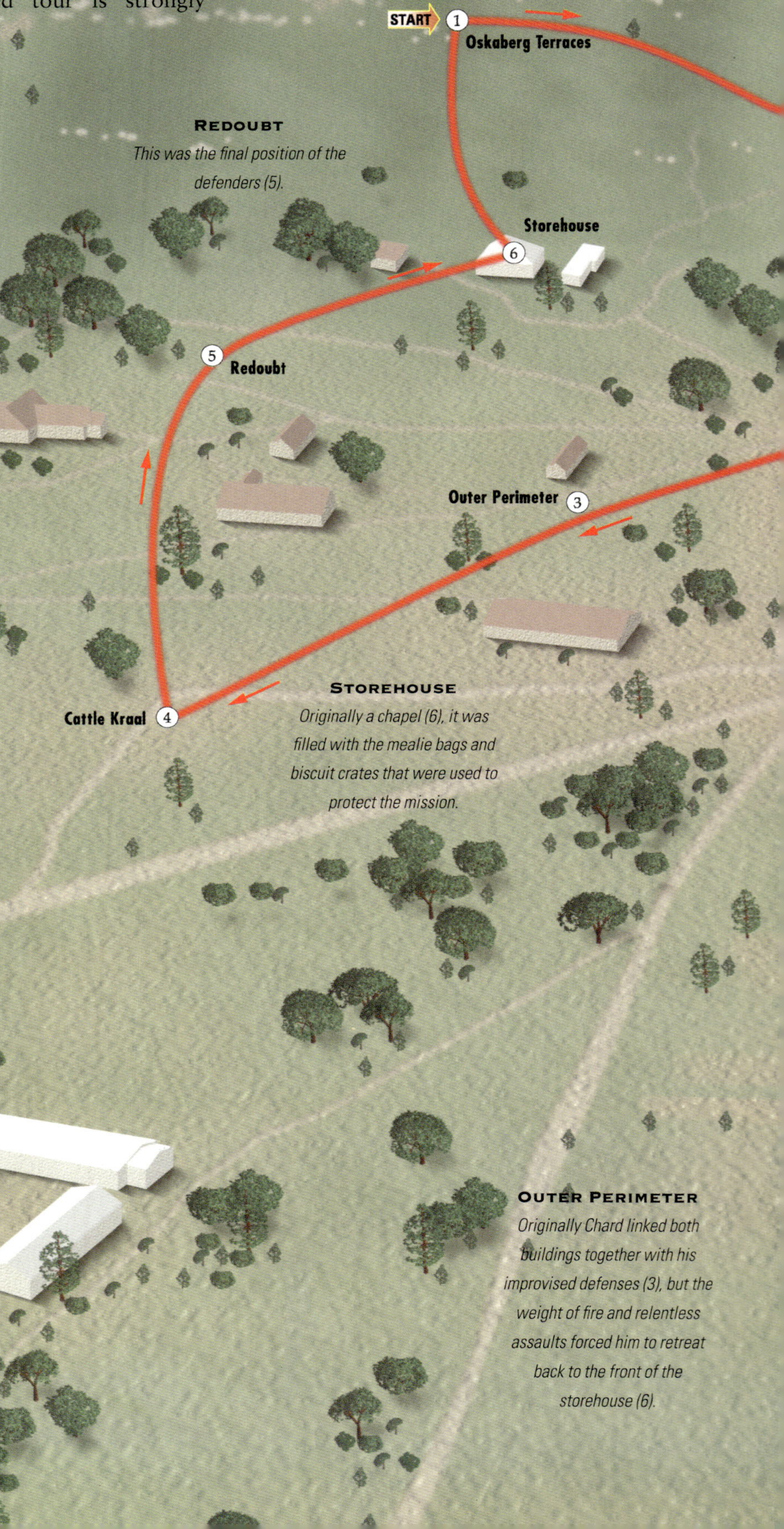

OSKARBERG TERRACES

The terraces (1) behind the mission were occupied by Zulu snipers who poured an effective fire into the British perimeter.

REDOUBT

This was the final position of the defenders (5).

STOREHOUSE

Originally a chapel (6), it was filled with the mealie bags and biscuit crates that were used to protect the mission.

OUTER PERIMETER

Originally Chard linked both buildings together with his improvised defenses (3), but the weight of fire and relentless assaults forced him to retreat back to the front of the storehouse (6).

BELOW ***Site of the mealie-bag redoubt*** *in front of the storehouse and last-stand position of the British.*

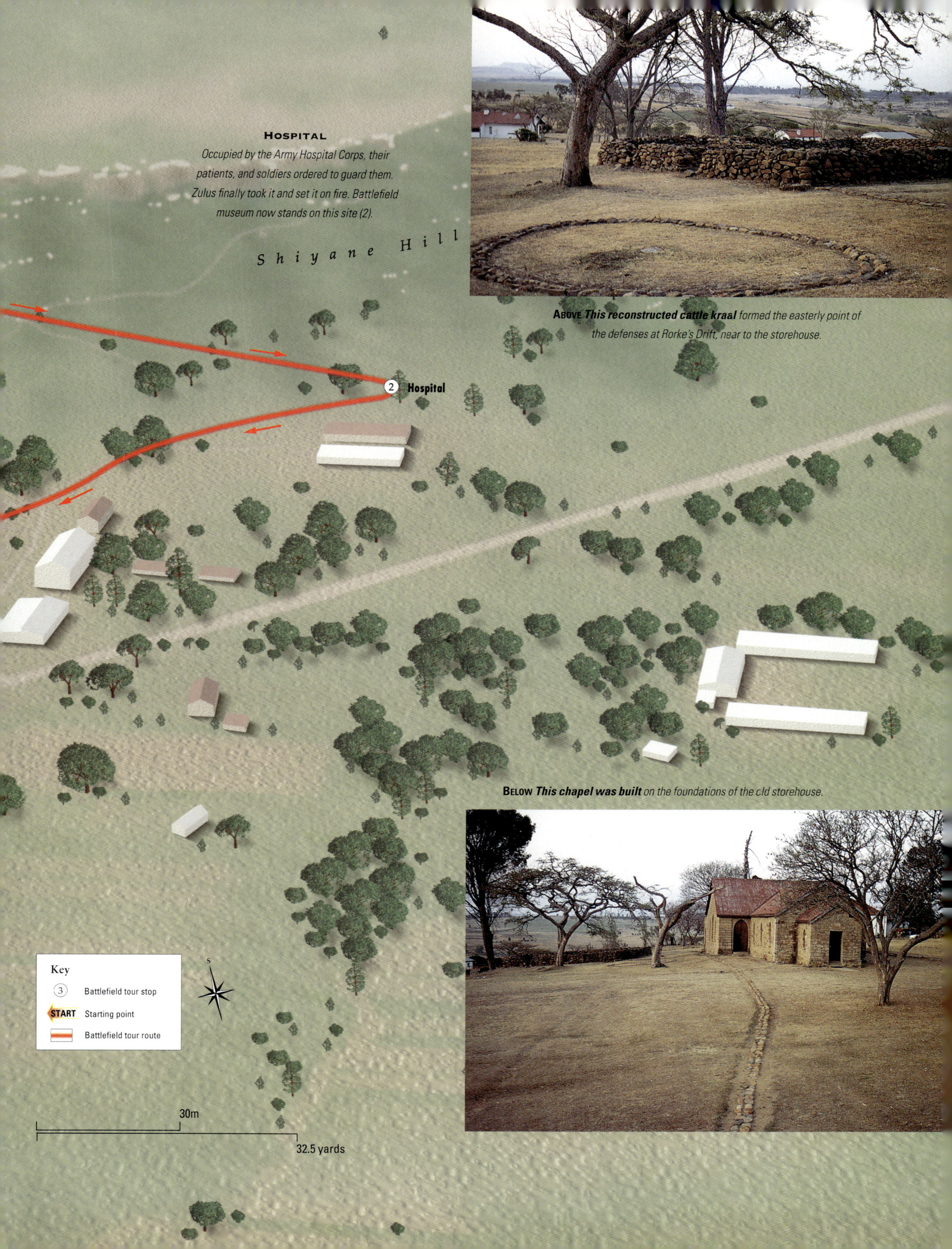

ABOVE *This reconstructed cattle kraal* *formed the easterly point of the defenses at Rorke's Drift, near to the storehouse.*

BELOW *This chapel was built* *on the foundations of the old storehouse.*

HELL IN THE PACIFIC

Above *Liberator's Memorial,* *Asan Beach, honoring veterans of the U.S. armed forces who participated in the 1944 landings.*

Left *U.S. troops emerge from a landing craft* *during an exercise. Amphibious assaults had been well practiced by the Marines by the time they reached Guam, but coral reefs proved a barrier to a smooth landing.*

Guam, along with Tinian and Saipan, is one of the larger islands in the Marianas island chain in the Pacific. As the U.S. army fought its way across the Pacific during World War II, these islands became strategically important, providing airbases for Boeing B-29 bombers so they could make round-trip raids on Japan. Possession of these islands would also cut the Japanese supply route across the Pacific. On top of this, there was one more reason for taking Guam—vengeance. Guam had been U.S. territory since 1898 and the Japanese had quickly captured it in 1941. Now, the Americans were coming back.

AMPHIBIOUS ASSAULT

Japan's conquest of Guam began barely an hour after their attack on Pearl Harbor. Japanese dive-bombers left Saipan and raked the lightly defended island for two days. A small defense force consisting of 153 Marines, 271 U.S. Navy, and 247 local Chamorro Guards were quickly overwhelmed by units of the Japanese army. Captain G. J. McMillin, the island's governor, saw little point in continuing the fighting and surrendered the island. The island natives now had to endure two and a half years of Japanese occupation in which the island was transformed

BACKGROUND TO BATTLE

The war in the Pacific began in 1941 with the surprise Japanese bombing raid on the U.S. battle fleet at Pearl Harbor. This was followed by the rapid Japanese capture of several Western possessions in Southeast Asia, including Malaya, Guam, Hong Kong, Singapore, and finally the Philippines. On June 6, 1942, the U.S. Navy halted the enemy, inflicting on the Japanese the first major defeat, at the battle of Midway. On August 7, the U.S. army intensified the war against the Japanese with their invasion of Guadalcanal in the Solomon Islands.

Island hopping became the method of choice for pursuing the war in 1943 against the Japanese, as the United States got closer and closer to Japan. In 1944, the noose tightened around Japan with B-29s bombing Tokyo from China. By February, the Marshall Islands had been captured and in March the Admiralty Islands are seized. In June, Saipan was invaded, but with suicidal resistance from the Japanese that made the U.S. despair of ending the war quickly. Between June 19 and 20, the battle of the Philippine Sea was fought. In an action nicknamed the Marianas Turkey Shoot, U.S. carrier-based aircraft inflicted crippling losses on Japanese carrier-based aircraft, thus ending Japanese naval dominance in the area. This paved the way for the invasion of Guam and Tinian.

into a Japanese colony with English forbidden and only Japanese taught at school. As the war began to move against Japan, conditions became even harsher on the island with many Chamorros being worked to death digging cave shelters for soldiers, while thousands of others languished in concentration camps.

By the summer of 1944, the U.S. armed forces were ready to turn their attention to rescuing the island of Guam. It was not going to be easy. The island was defended by 18,500 Japanese soldiers dug in to strongly prepared defensive positions. The U.S. army, however, had well practiced its methods of amphibious warfare and mustered some 55,000 men from the 3rd Marine Division, 1st Provisional Marine Brigade, and the 305th Regimental Combat Team of the 77th Army's Infantry Division. The assault began with one of the heaviest preparatory naval bombardments of the war, lasting an entire seventeen days.

When the shattering fire ceased on July 21, U.S. Marines streamed toward the beaches in their landing craft. The Japanese scrambled out of their bunkers and caves and inflicted heavy fire on the incoming troops. The first wave of Marines landed on a beach west of Agana, enduring mortar fire as they pushed through dried paddy fields to win a wide beachhead that cost over 700 casualties. South of the Orote Peninsula, near Agat, twenty-four landing craft were destroyed and more than 350 casualties inflicted on Americans landing there. Island reefs hampered the landings and one rifleman recalls "a long wade to the beach, searching for footing on the treacherous coral bottom, wrestling with our equipment, sometimes up to our necks in water." By dusk, they had reached the slopes of Mount Alifan, bringing in tanks to hammer the Japanese defenders. The Japanese

LEFT *Sculpted bronze panels* *depict scenes of the U.S. landing, occupation, and liberation of Guam. Located within the Memorial Wall at Asan Bay Overlook.*

BACKGROUND *U.S. Marines take shelter on the beach* *during the landings at Guam. They encountered stiff resistance from Japanese soldiers protected by stone and steel gun emplacements.*

SUICIDAL DETERMINATION

Although by the summer of 1944 the United States was beginning to turn around the war against Japan, there was a sinking feeling among many of the armed forces that the Japanese would not easily accept the shift in power. Suicidal defenses of their islands against U.S. assaults made sickening news, as Snelling Robinson, a young ensign on the destroyer U.S.S. *Cotten*, recalls:

"It was now all but certain that there would be no further intervention by Japanese naval forces in the Marianas area. The failure of their navy to assist them did not mean, however, that the Japanese forces on Guam and Tinian would not continue to fight…The Japanese on Saipan had literally fought to the finish. At the end of the campaign there had been some four thousand Japanese troops left of the twenty-two thousand effectives at the start, not counting those hidden in the hills. These four thousand had made a final attack that for its ferocity was unprecedented. By the time the attack was over, every Japanese participant was dead. With this knowledge of the enemy, no one in the Pacific Fleet or the Marine Corps felt at this time that the Japanese believed they could be defeated. On the contrary, the end still seemed as distant as it had been when the *Cotten* had entered the Pacific area some ten months previously."

Quoted in 200,000 MILES ABOARD THE DESTROYER COTTEN *by C. Snelling Robinson (Kent State University Press, 2000).*

U.S. Marine, waiting in a landing craft, *has his face blackened to serve as camouflage before hitting the beaches at Guam. Other soldiers wear more conventional camouflaged helmet covers and tunic first introduced into the U.S. army to be worn by Marines in the Pacific War.*

counterattacked fiercely with explosives and suicidal bayonet charges, but by the next morning 600 of them were dead.

WORSE TO COME

With the capture of Mount Alifan, the Marines thrust inland and toward the Orote Peninsula. This meant struggling through dense undergrowth and swamps, constantly being assaulted by Japanese armed with mortars, mines, tanks, and artillery. But worse was to come. On the evening of July 25, after having carefully reconnoitered the American positions to discern their weakest point, the Japanese launched a massive counterattack from the mountains south of Asan Point, west of Agana. Japanese, drunk on sake, became human bombs as they pierced the lines of the Marines loaded with explosives. "Wake up Americans and die!" they yelled in English. The fighting was at close quarters and desperate as the Japanese used any weapons to hand, including baseball bats and pitchforks. A field hospital was overrun and wounded Marines were forced into a bitter fight for survival.

ABOVE *View of the Asan Invasion Beach* *where the Third Marine Division landed on July 21, 1944.*

BELOW *U.S. Marines pose for an official photograph* *during jungle fighting in the Pacific. Note the cameraman in the foreground.*

Captain Louis H. Wilson, Jr. of F Company, 2nd Battalion, 9th Marines, had been wounded three times the previous day, but left his medical aid station to join the fighting, leading his men throughout the night in close combat. He then led a group of seventeen men, thirteen of whom became casualties, to capture vital high ground. He was one of four Marines to be awarded the Medal of Honor for bravery in this fighting.

The morning after the counterattack, the 3rd Marine Division was surrounded by 3,200 dead Japanese. They had suffered 600 casualties. It had been a trauma and the worst was over, but Japanese defenders fought on for several more days, even after their commander, Lieutenant General Takeshi, was killed. Eventually, on August 10, Guam's northern coast finally fell to the Americans and the Stars and Stripes flew once more over their island. It had been a costly battle. The U.S. army had 1,744 dead and 5,970 wounded. Only 1,250 Japanese were captured alive; more than 17,000 had been killed or were missing. In a bizarre twist, a few Japanese held out in the jungle of Guam for years afterwards—two surrendering as late as 1967 and one in 1972.

BEACHES IN GUAM

AGAT AND ASAN BEACHES are preserved today as part of the War in the Pacific National Historical Park in Guam. The fighting at Agat beach, south of Orote Peninsula, was particularly intense on the first day of landing with the U.S. Marines suffering more than 1,000 casualties. As their landing vehicles approached the beach across the wide reef at Agat, they were raked by mortar and artillery fire. As the Marines waded onto the beach, machines guns emplaced at Ga'an Point opened fire, forestalling the prospect of any successful frontal assault. The gun emplacements were eventually knocked out by U.S. tanks attacking them from the rear. Japanese fortifications at Ga'an Point can still be seen today alongside some of the guns used by the Japanese.

Japanese soldiers *invade a Pacific island. Japanese wartime painting by Ezaki Kohei.*

The landings on Asan beach were less heavily challenged, and the U.S. Marines moved inland, establishing a beachhead and forcing the Japanese to retreat to Fonte Plateau and Mount Chachao. Many Japanese survived the prelanding bombardment by sheltering in a cave system along Asan Ridge. Because of the bombardment and heavy rain, the Asan area was a sea of mud, and many Marines suffered from heat and exhaustion as they clambered through the heavy undergrowth. When the fierce Japanese counterattack came, it focused on Asan Point but, despite several suicidal assaults, the U.S. line held. Several Japanese gun emplacements and tunnels can now be seen at Asan point, alongside memorials to the Marines that died.

Overall, there are seven different areas forming the National Historical Park on Guam, and other areas worth seeing include the Piti Guns, Japanese coastal defense guns, that lie near the Guam Veterans' Cemetery.

PLAN OF BATTLE

The liberation of Guam in 1944 began with a massive naval and aerial bombardment that lasted seventeen days. This was then followed by amphibious landings at two major points near Agat and Asan, the main target being to secure the Orote Peninsula with its airstrip. Having captured this by July 29, U.S. forces then advanced northward along the island, encountering stiff Japanese resistance in jungles and swamps.

GUAM

GUAM IS A BEAUTIFUL TROPICAL ISLAND in which coral reefs rich with wildlife can be visited alongside several areas and memorials commemorating its U.S. liberation in 1944. Asan Point is one of seven areas forming the War in the Pacific National Historical Park on Guam.

Coral Reef
Turquoise water reveals a wonderful array of tropical fish, but this coral formed a barrier during the U.S. landings at Asan that made it difficult for troops to get ashore

GETTING THERE

Location: *Guam, Mariana Islands, Pacific.*

Visitor Information: *National Park Service, War in the Pacific National Historical Park, 115 Marine Drive, Haloda Building, Asan, Guam 96922.*

Telephone: *671 477 9362*

Directions: *International flight to island capital of Agana, then short drive west to Asan Point.*

Tour Distance: *33 miles (59km).*

Landing Beaches
U.S. troops landed at both Ga'an Point (5) and Asan Point (7) where there are now several monuments lining the beach.

Above *Japanese 8 inch (20cm) naval gun* *located at Ga'an Point, scene of fierce fire directed at the landing U.S. Marines.*

Above *Japanese coastal defense gun* *at Piti Guns historic trail.*

Japanese Tunnel

Dug by the forced labor of the local Chamorros, such tunnels as the one near Asan Point (7), sheltered the Japanese soldiers during the lengthy prelanding bombardment.

Gun Emplacements

Steel gun bases (3), dug into the limestone rock, formed part of the Japanese defenses of Guam.

Left *Ga'an Point, site of the southern landing beach,* *now flies three flags in honor of the American, Guamanian, and Japanese casualties of the fighting there.*

TET OFFENSIVE

Above *First Air Cavalry helicopter* *delivers men to the front in Vietnam. Helicopter support was vital for the Marines in Hue and for transporting reinforcements into the center of the city.*

Left *U.S. machine gunner* *lays down heavy fire during the conflict with the NVA. Small arms such as assault rifles, machine guns, and grenades were the main forms of weapon used in Hue, as neither side wanted to destroy the historic city; but the ferocity of the fighting eventually led to the use of artillery and air strikes.*

TET WAS THE VIETNAMESE NEW YEAR holiday and was traditionally a period of celebration and truce. In North Vietnam, however, in January 1968, the holiday was brought forward a day. Three days later, the North Vietnamese launched a massive assault on South Vietnam, while the South Vietnamese were still enjoying their Tet holiday. Some 80,000 soldiers of the North Vietnam Army (NVA) and the Vietcong (VC) attacked thirty-six of the forty-four provincial capitals. The Americans and the South Vietnamese were caught off guard, but fought back strongly. Over a period of two weeks, some 32,000 North Vietnamese were killed and most thrown back, but in Hue the fighting continued.

MARINE RESCUE

Hue was the third-largest city in South Vietnam and was once the capital of French Indo-China. At the heart of the city, on the northern bank of the Perfume River, was the nearly two-mile square walled Citadel, housing the old city and the Imperial Palace. It had avoided heavy fighting so far, as both sides respected its historical and cultural significance, but all that was to change. During Tet in 1968, Communist soldiers infiltrated the civilians of Hue and quickly took over the city. Vo Nguyen Giap, the North Vietnamese commander, committed nine battalions to the capture of Hue.

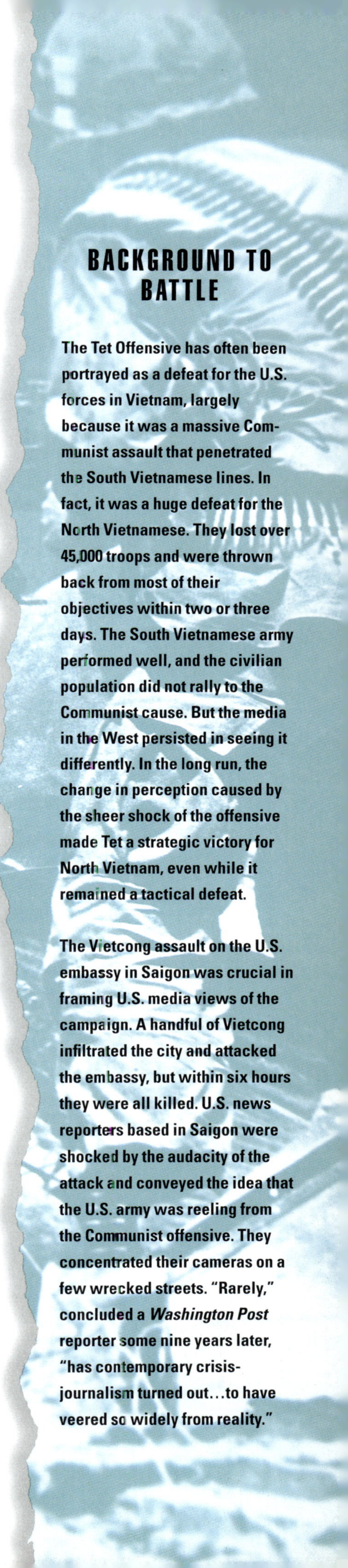

BACKGROUND TO BATTLE

The Tet Offensive has often been portrayed as a defeat for the U.S. forces in Vietnam, largely because it was a massive Communist assault that penetrated the South Vietnamese lines. In fact, it was a huge defeat for the North Vietnamese. They lost over 45,000 troops and were thrown back from most of their objectives within two or three days. The South Vietnamese army performed well, and the civilian population did not rally to the Communist cause. But the media in the West persisted in seeing it differently. In the long run, the change in perception caused by the sheer shock of the offensive made Tet a strategic victory for North Vietnam, even while it remained a tactical defeat.

The Vietcong assault on the U.S. embassy in Saigon was crucial in framing U.S. media views of the campaign. A handful of Vietcong infiltrated the city and attacked the embassy, but within six hours they were all killed. U.S. news reporters based in Saigon were shocked by the audacity of the attack and conveyed the idea that the U.S. army was reeling from the Communist offensive. They concentrated their cameras on a few wrecked streets. "Rarely," concluded a *Washington Post* reporter some nine years later, "has contemporary crisis-journalism turned out...to have veered so widely from reality."

Inside the city were a handful of South Vietnamese troops and their American advisers of the Military Assistance Command Vietnam (MACV). The Americans hit back at the NVA with some success, but they were small in numbers and trapped in the MACV compound.

Reinforcements from Marine headquarters at Phu Bai rushed north along Highway 1 to Hue, but they were hastily put together by Captain Gordon D. Batcheller, commander of Alpha Company, 1st Battalion, 1st Marine Regiment, and consisted of only eighty Marines, some South Vietnamese soldiers, and a column of four Marine M-48 tanks, a jeep, and a mobile crane. Once in the city, the little rescue group was ambushed by the NVA, coming under heavy fire that seriously wounded Batcheller. They bravely attempted to reach the American compound, but were halted. More Marines under Lieutenant Colonel Marcus J. Gravel, commander of the 1st Battalion, 1st Marines, now surged out of Phu Bai to reinforce these troops. Charging the NVA positions, the Marines forced their way through to the MACV compound.

Inside the Citadel, the headquarters of the South Vietnamese Army (ARVN headquarters) was under siege. Brigadier General Ngo Quang Truong, commander of the ARVN 1st Division, ordered more reinforcements to join him from outside the city and they battered their way through the NVA to reach their commander. The tide was beginning to turn against the NVA.

Helicopters brought in two more Marine battalions to a football field near the MACV

Below *Entrance to the historic walled Citadel* *at Hue. The walls and moat surrounding it were built with help from the French in the nineteenth century. (Photo by Kieran Lynch.)*

LEFT *U.S. Marines fight* *through the streets of Hue against the North Vietnamese during the Tet Offensive.*

compound and they began to fight their way north toward the Citadel. The NVA hoped to ambush motorized columns by placing their men in buildings on either side of a street, but the Marines avoided this threat by using explosives to blast holes in the sides of buildings and take streets house by house. Within ten days of this kind of deadly close fighting, the Marines had recaptured the southern part of the city, but the South Vietnamese in the Citadel were still having difficulties with the NVA.

FIGHTING IN THE CITADEL

The South Vietnamese were put in a terrible situation by the fighting in the Citadel. Many of them had their own families in houses within the ancient walls and one South Vietnamese artillery soldier was in tears as he had to order artillery fire onto his own house, knowing his family were sheltering inside. After a week of this desperate fighting, the South Vietnamese army

COMMUNIST ATROCITIES

Mark W. Woodruff was an antitank assaultman with the Third Marine Regiment during the Tet Offensive in 1968. He later wrote a book in which he described the terrible atrocities against South Vietnamese civilians by the Vietcong during their occupation of Hue:

"On the fifth day of the Communist occupation [of Hue], the Vietcong came to Phu Cam Cathedral and gathered together 400 men and boys. Some were identified by name from their lists, others because they were of military age, and still others simply because they looked wealthy. They were last seen being marched away to the south. Two years later, three Vietcong defectors led troops of the 101st Airborne Division to a creek bed in the dense jungle ten miles from Hue. Spread out for a hundred meters were the bones of the men and boys of Phu Cam. The number murdered was later confirmed as 428 . . . Some had been shot, others had been clubbed to death . . . The bloodletting continued for days until the North Vietnamese army commander learned of the Vietcong's actions and put a stop to it. A total of 2,810 bodies were eventually found in shallow mass graves; 1,946 people remained unaccounted for."

From UNHERALDED VICTORY *by Mark W. Woodruff (HarperCollins, 2000).*

U.S. antiwar poster parodying *the Uncle Sam recruitment poster of World War I. The Tet Offensive was seized upon by the U.S. media as an American failure, but it was, in fact, a catastrophic defeat for the North Vietnamese.*

decided to withdraw within their own headquarters compound. General Truong now had to admit he could not recapture the Citadel by himself and had to request that Americans help him. Giap, in the meantime, had to shift five more battalions to help with his hold on Hue. The Tet Offensive was failing and draining men from the NVA.

Marines were helicoptered directly into the ARVN headquarters within the Citadel while others crowded into landing craft that steamed along the Perfume River toward the ancient walls. South Vietnamese civilians warned the Marines from the boats of an NVA ambush and led them safely into the Citadel. Once inside, the Americans now pushed the NVA southward to the river, so they were trapped between two American forces. Having got permission from the South Vietnamese to use artillery and air strikes, they could now improve their firepower too. By February 23, the NVA commander was given permission to withdraw from Hue.

The Marines had now virtually cleared out the whole of the Citadel except for the Imperial Palace, which remained in the hands of the NVA. Readying themselves for a final assault, they were told that the South Vietnamese would take it instead. With their U.S. adviser at the front, the elite Black Panther unit charged across the courtyard, firing their rifles while carrying ladders to haul themselves over the walls. Most of the NVA had already gone. The Black Panthers pulled down the Communist flag and raised their own. In total, the NVA had lost 5,000 soldiers within the walls of Hue. The Americans suffered 1,000 casualties (119 killed) and the ARVN nearly twice that.

Above *U.S. military adviser* *instructs South Vietnamese soldier in the use of a grenade launcher. The South Vietnamese army performed bravely during the battle for Hue, but eventually needed the help of the U.S. Marines to clear the old city.*

Below *Imperial Palace courtyard,* *across which the South Vietnamese Black Panther unit charged to capture the palace from the NVA. (Photo by Kieran Lynch.)*

HUE

Ho Chi Minh, *political leader of the North Vietnamese Army.*

The Citadel at Hue is a beautiful complex of palaces and temples that was respected by both sides during the fighting in Vietnam, until the North Vietnamese invaded its walls and all hell broke loose. The South Vietnamese were eventually forced to use artillery and air strikes on their own precious, ancient city. Much of the Citadel, including its surrounding walls and moats was constructed with French help in the nineteenth century when it became the capital of French Indo-China. Today, many of the buildings within the Citadel are still being restored long after the fighting in 1968.

The physical structure of the city of Hue dictated much of the fighting that took place. The NVA had infiltrated the area and quickly constructed strongpoints every few blocks. Buildings within Hue are typically surrounded by courtyards, and the NVA dug one-man holes in them, each holding a soldier armed with an AK-47 assault rifle and an RPG anti-tank rocket. Machine-gun teams were then placed in the lower story of the house inside the courtyard with snipers in the two upper stories. It was a defense designed to ensnare South Vietnamese armored columns that might enter the city to relieve their headquarters. Fire from the strongpoints would engulf the vehicles and shatter the columns.

U.S. forces did not fall into these traps, and opted for the more difficult tactic of taking each strongpoint. At first, the Marines used smoke grenades to screen their attacks, but the NVA knew this was the prelude to an assault and set up a ferocious storm of fire. The Marines quickly adapted by using smoke grenades to draw fire and identify enemy positions. They then used recoilless rifles to smash into the NVA positions, while their main force advanced behind the shooting to attack the buildings by blowing holes through the walls into the courtyards and houses. As the Marines broke into a building, the NVA would frequently evacuate, but the Marines covered this by lobbing mortar fire to the rear of buildings they attacked. It was laborious, lethal fighting, but slowly and surely the Marines recaptured the city this way.

PLAN OF BATTLE

The battle for Hue began with NVA and VC infiltrators taking over the city on the night of January 31, 1968. American advisers were surrounded in the MACV compound, and South Vietnamese forces besieged in the ARVN headquarters inside the Citadel. The MACV compound was relieved by U.S. Marines and this became a stepping-off point for clearing NVA forces from the southern half of the city. After hard fighting in the Citadel, the South Vietnamese withdrew into their headquarters and asked for U.S. help to clear out the walled city. The Imperial Palace fell on February 21, and the city went back into U.S. and South Vietnamese hands.

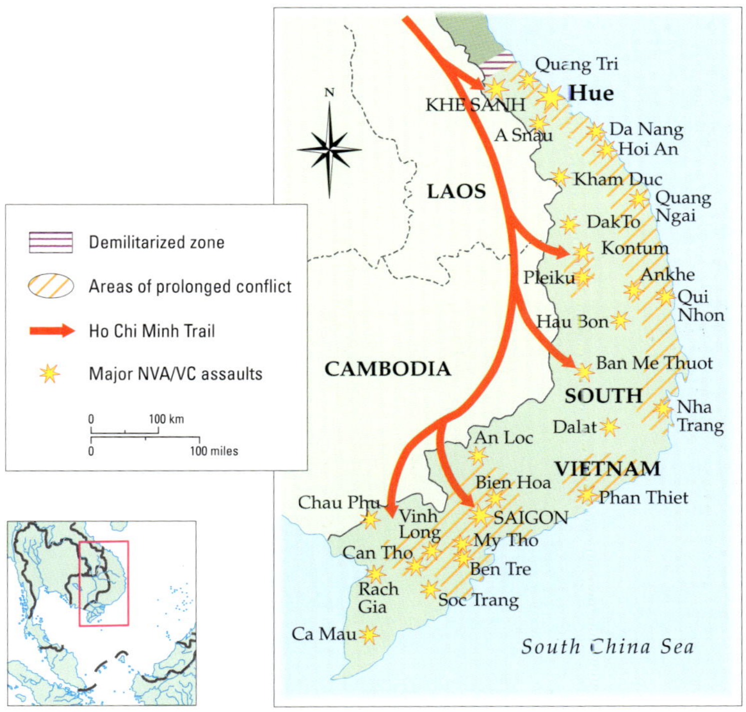

HUE

HUE IS ONE OF THE LARGEST CITIES in central Vietnam and one of the most interesting, with the picturesque Citadel and old city at its heart. Travel inside Vietnam is cheap and readily available, but an organized battlefield tour is probably the best way to visit the city.

ARVN HEADQUARTERS

Inside the Citadel (3), this was the main South Vietnamese position from which they attacked the NVA in the Citadel and eventually withdrew inside, calling for U.S. help.

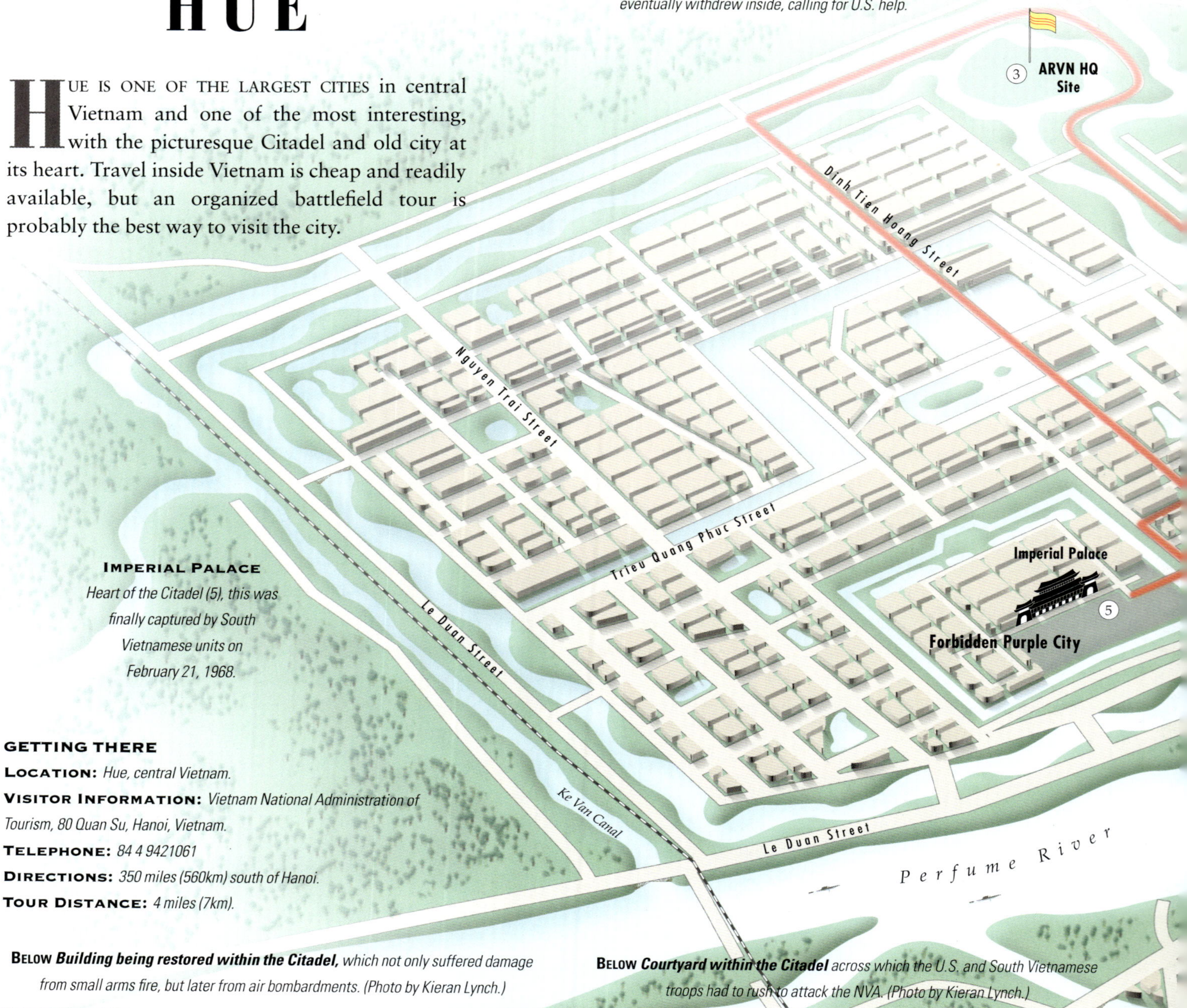

IMPERIAL PALACE

Heart of the Citadel (5), this was finally captured by South Vietnamese units on February 21, 1968.

GETTING THERE

LOCATION: *Hue, central Vietnam.*

VISITOR INFORMATION: *Vietnam National Administration of Tourism, 80 Quan Su, Hanoi, Vietnam.*

TELEPHONE: *84 4 9421061*

DIRECTIONS: *350 miles (560km) south of Hanoi.*

TOUR DISTANCE: *4 miles (7km).*

BELOW ***Building being restored within the Citadel,*** *which not only suffered damage from small arms fire, but later from air bombardments. (Photo by Kieran Lynch.)*

BELOW ***Courtyard within the Citadel*** *across which the U.S. and South Vietnamese troops had to rush to attack the NVA. (Photo by Kieran Lynch.)*

Above ***Bullet damage from 1968*** *still remains in a wall in the Citadel at Hue. (Photo by Kieran Lynch.)*

TOUR OPERATORS, ORGANIZATIONS, AND MUSEUMS

BATTLEFIELD TOUR OPERATORS

BATTLEFIELDS AFRICA
Box 2388, Hillcrest 2350, South Africa
Contact: Ron Lock
Fax: 031 765 1244
Zulu, Boer and South African Wars, professional guide.

BATTLEFIELD TOURS (U.S.A.)
304 Lookout Drive, Rising Fawn, GA 30738-2261, U.S.A.
Website: battlefields.home.mindspring.com
Telephone: 706 398 0962
Detailed tours of the Chickamauga and Chattanooga battlefields.

BATTLEFIELD TOURS (FRANCE)
17 rue de l'Eglise, 62134, Pas de Calais, Predifin, France.
Website: www.euro-traveller.com
Contact: Malcolm Carpenter
Telephone: 03 2104 9579
Fully guided tours in Northern France and Belgium, including Vimy Ridge.

CONNECTIONS GROUP TOURS
101 Duncan Mill Road, Suite 305, Don Mills, Ontario, M3B 1Z3, Canada
Website: www.connectiongrouptours.com
Telephone: 416 449 4652; 877 449 4652
Fax: 416 449 9965
Focuses on North America's involvement in World War I and World War II in Europe.

CUSTER BATTLEFIELD TOURS
P.O. Box 310, Hardin, MT 59034, U.S.A.
Website: www.actiontravelmontana.com
Contact: Jim Court
Telephone: 406 665 1580
Fax: 406 665 3133
All-day tours following Custer's route at the Battle of Little Bighorn.

GUAM SAFARI TOURS
3 Hibiscus Lane, Ipan, Talofofo, GU 96930
Website: www.guam.net/home/guamsafari
Telephone: 671 789 1996
Fax: 671 789 1993
Tours of Guam including World War II battlefields.

HISTORIC TOURS
1281 Paterson Plank Road, Secaucus, NJ 07094, U.S.A.
Website: www.WW2tours.com
Telephone: 800 222 1170
Operates World War II and Cold War historic tours of Europe and Australia.

HOLTS TOURS (BATTLEFIELDS & HISTORY)
The Old Plough, High Street, Eastry, CT13 OHF, U.K.
Website: www.battletours.co.uk
Contact: John Hughes-Wilson
Telephone: 01304 612248
Fax: 01304 614930
Military historical tour operator, with programs spanning history from the Romans to the Falklands War. Especially well known for World War I and World War II battlefield tours.

IAN FLETCHER BATTLEFIELD TOURS
P.O. Box 112, Rochester, Kent ME1 2EX, U.K.
Website: www.ifbt.co.uk
Contact: Ian Fletcher
Telephone: 01634 319973
Fax: 01634 324263
Peninsular War and Waterloo tours.

MIDAS HISTORICAL TOURS LTD
The Ravelin, Sheperd's Hill, Buckhorn Weston, Dorset, SP8 5HZ, U.K.
Website: www.midastours.co.uk
Contact: Alan Rooney
Telephone: 01963 371550
Fax: 01963 371510
Escorted tours covering ancient and medieval warfare, Napoleonic, American Civil War, South Africa, India, Crimea, World War I, and World War II.

MIDDLEBROOK-HODGSON BATTLEFIELD TOURS
48 Linden Way, Boston, Lincolnshire PE21 9DS, U.K.
Telephone: 01526 342249
Fax: 01526 345249
Tours to World War I's Western Front, Ypres to Verdun, Normandy, Gallipoli.

NINE DRAGON TOURS
Glendale Center Mall, 6101 North Keystone Avenue, Indianapolis, IN 46220-2431, U.S.A.
Website: www.nine-dragons.com
Telephone: 317 329 0350
Fax: 317 329 0117
Organizes tours of the battlefields in Vietnam, including Hue.

OLD COUNTRY TOURS INC.
10737 Piney Island Drive, Bishopville, Maryland 21813, U.S.A.
Website: www.oldcountrytours.com
Telephone: 410 352 3639
Fax: 410 352 5739
Tours of historical battlefields in the U.S. and Europe.

SOMME BATTLEFIELD TOURS LTD
19 Old Road, Wimborne, Dorset, BH21 1EJ, U.K.
Website: www.btinternet.com/~sommetours
Contact: James Power
Telephone/Fax: 01202 840520
Specializes in taking small groups to all the major sites as well as off the beaten track around the battlefields of the Somme, Ypres, and Verdun.

UK TOURS & TRAVEL
34 Bradford Avenue, Bolton, Lancashire BL1 8HF, U.K.
Contact: Peter and Angela Smith
Telephone/Fax: 01204 384940
American Civil War battlefield tours.

THE WAR RESEARCH SOCIETY BATTLEFIELD AND MEMORIAL PILGRIMAGE TOURS
The War Research Society, 27 Courtway Avenue, Birmingham B14 4PP, U.K.
Website: www.battlefieldtours.co.uk
Contact: Ian C. Alexander
Telephone: 0121 4305348
Fax: 0121 4367401
Battlefield tours all over Europe and of the Boer/Zulu wars battlefields.

BATTLEFIELD ORGANIZATIONS

ENGLISH HERITAGE
23 Saville Row, London W1X 2ET, U.K.
Telephone: 020 7973 3460
Administers English battlefields and organizes events on these sites.

NATIONAL PARK SERVICE
1849 C Street NW, Washington D.C. 20240, U.S.A.
Website: www.nps.gov
Telephone: 202 208 6843
Administers U.S. National Military Parks.

BATTLEFIELD MUSEUMS

AUSTRALIA

SOUTH AUSTRALIA MILITARY VEHICLE MUSEUM
252 Commercial Road, Port Adelaide,
South Australia, 5015
Website: www.military-vehicle-museum.org.au
Telephone: 61 8 8341 3011

CANADA

BATTLEFIELD HOUSE MUSEUM
77 King Street West, P.O. Box 66561, Stoney Creek,
Ontario, L8G 3X9
Website: alpha.binatech.on.ca/~bhmchin
Telephone: 905 662 8458
Fax: 905 662 0529

CANADIAN WAR MUSEUM
General Motors Court, 330 Sussex Drive, Ottowa,
Ontario, K1A 0M8
Website: www.warmuseum.ca
Telephone: 819 776 8600
Fax: 819 776 8623

FRANCE

MUSEE DE LA TARGETTE
48, rue Nationale, 62580 Neuville St Vaast
Telephone/Fax: 03 21 59 17 76

HISTORIAL DE LA GRANDE GUERRE
Chateau de Péronne, B.P. 63-8020, Peronne
Cedex
Telephone: 03 22 83 14 18
Fax: 03 22 83 54 18

MUSEE MEMORIAL DE FLEURY
Fleury-devant-Douaumont, 55100, Verdun
Telephone: 03 29 84 35 34
Fax: 03 29 84 45 54

GERMANY

ALLIED MUSEUM
Clayallee 135, Outpost, 14195, Berlin, Zehlendorf
Website: www.alliiertenmuseum.de
Telephone: 30 81 81 990
Fax: 30 81 81 99 91

HOLLAND

ARNHEM WAR MUSEUM 40-45
Kemperbergerweg 780-6816 RX, Arnhem (Schaarsbergen),
The Netherlands.
Telephone: 03 29 84 35 34
Fax: 03 29 84 45 54

POLAND

HISTORICAL MUSEUM OF THE CAPITAL CITY OF WARSAW
Muzeum Miasta Stolecznego Warszawa, Rynek Starego,
Miasta 28/42, 00-272 Warszawa
Telephone: 22 635 1625
Fax: 22 25 85 59

SOUTH AFRICA

ANGLO-BOER WAR MUSEUM
100 Monument Road, Bloemfontein, 9301
Website: www.anglo-boer.co.za
Telephone: 27 51 447 3447
Fax: 27 51 447 1322

SOUTH AFRICAN MUSEUM OF MILITARY HISTORY
Zoo Lake, Johannesburg
Telephone: 27 11 646 5513

TALANA MUSEUM
P.B. 2024, Dundee, 3000
Telephone: 034 212 2654
Website: www.talana.co.za

TURKEY

MILITARY MUSEUM
Valikonagoi, C 80200, Nis Antas, Istanbul
Telephone: 212 223 27 20

NAVAL MUSEUM
Cimenlik Kalesi (Cimenlik Park), Canakkale
Telephone: 286 862 00 82

U.K.

IMPERIAL WAR MUSEUM
Lambeth Road, London, SE1 6HZ
Website: www.iwm.org.uk
Telephone: 020 7416 5320
Fax: 020 7416 5374

BRITAIN AT WAR EXPERIENCE
64-66 Tooley Street, London Bridge, London, SE1 2TF
Website: www.britainatwar.co.uk
Telephone: 020 7403 3171
Fax: 020 7403 5104

REGIMENTAL MUSEUM OF THE ARGYLL AND SUTHERLAND HIGHLANDERS
The Castle, Stirling FK8 1EH, Scotland
Telephone: 01786 475165

U.S.A.

CHICKAMAUGA AND CHATTANOOGA NATIONAL MILITARY PARK MUSEUM
P.O. Box 2128, Fort Oglethorpe, GA 30742
Website: www.nps.gov/chch
Telephone: 615 752 5213

CIVIL WAR SOLDIERS MUSEUM
108 South Palafox Place, Pensacola, FL 32501
Website: cwmuseum.org
Telephone: 850 469 1900, *Fax*: 850 469 9328

THE CONFEDERATE MUSEUM
929 Camp Street, New Orleans, LA 70130
Website: www.confederatemuseum.com
Telephone: 504 523 4522
Fax: 504 523 8595

CUSTER BATTLEFIELD MUSEUM
Town Hall, P.O. Box 200, Garryowen, MT 59031
Website: www.custermuseum.org
Telephone: 406 638 1876

LITTLE BIGHORN BATTLEFIELD MUSEUM
P.O. Box 39, Crow Agency, MT 59022
Telephone: 406 638 2621

MILITARY VEHICLE MUSEUM
1918 North Rosemead Boulevard, South El Monte, CA
Telephone: 626 442 1776
Fax: 626 443 1776

THE MUSEUM OF THE CONFEDERACY
1201 East Clay Street, Richmond, VA 23219
Website: www.moc.org
Telephone: 804 649 1861

NATIONAL MUSEUM OF CIVIL WAR MEDICINE
P.O. Box 470, Frederick, MD 21705
Website: www.civilwarmed.org
Telephone: 301 695 1864

OLD COURT HOUSE MUSEUM
Court Square, Vicksburg, MS 39183
Website: www.oldcourthouse.org
Telephone: 601 636 0741

PENNSYLVANIA MILITARY MUSEUM
P.O. Box 160A, Boalsburg, PA 16827
Website: www.psu.edu/dept/aerospace/museum
Telephone: 814 466 6263

INDEX

Page numbers in *italics* refer to captions

CREDITS

Pictures researched by Tim Newark.

Special thanks to Peter Newark's Military Pictures for providing the historical illustrations.

Thanks to the following photographers for supplying pictures: Alec Hasenson (pages 16-18, 20, 21, 24, 28, 33, 34, 36, 37, 39, 45), Kieran Lynch (pages 148, 150, 152, 153), Stephen Turnbull (pages 57, 59-62), Ian Knight (134-136), and Patrick Mercer (123-125, 128, 129).

Pictures also supplied by Pictures Colour Library (page 92).

Quarto Publishing would like to thank Ian Howes for the photography of Europe's battlefields.

The author, Tim Newark, would like to thank Ron Field and Andrzej Brzozowski for their help with the research.